Income
Distribution
and
Redistribution

PERSPECTIVES ON ECONOMICS SERIES

Michael L. Wachter & Susan M. Wachter, Editors

PUBLISHED

International Economic Order & Commodity Agreements, *Jere R. Behrman*
Labor Unions, *George H. Hildebrand*
Economics of Health, *Joseph Newhouse*
Monetarism, *William Poole*
Antitrust, *Roger Sherman*
Income Distribution and Redistribution, *Paul J. Taubman*

AVAILABLE IN FALL, 1978

The Fed and the Public Interest, *Edward J. Kane*
Forecasting, *Lawrence R. Klein & Michael M. Young*
Regulation, *Roger G. Noll*
Population, *T. Paul Schultz*
Inflation, *Michael L. Wachter*
Urban Economics, *Susan M. Wachter*

Income Distribution and Redistribution

Paul Taubman
University of Pennsylvania

ADDISON-WESLEY PUBLISHING COMPANY
Reading, Massachusetts • Menlo Park, California
London • Amsterdam • Don Mills, Ontario • Sydney

ISBN 0-201-08362-0
ABCDEFGHIJK-AL-798

Foreword

The PERSPECTIVES ON ECONOMICS series has been developed to present economics students with up-to-date policy-oriented books written by leading scholars in this field. Many professors and students have stressed the need for flexible, contemporary materials that provide an understanding of current policy issues.

In general, beginning students in economics are not exposed to the controversial material and development of current issues that are the basis of research in economics. Because of their length and breadth of coverage, textbooks tend to lack current economic thinking on policy questions; in attempting to provide a balanced viewpoint, they often do not give the reader a feel for the lively controversy in each field. With this series, we have attempted to fill this void.

The books in this series are designed to complement standard textbooks. Each volume reflects the research interests and views of the authors. Thus these books can also serve as basic reading material in the specific topic courses covered by each. The stress throughout is on the careful development of institutional factors and policy in the context of economic theory. Yet the exposition is designed to be accessible to undergraduate students and interested laypersons with an elementary background in economics.

Michael L. Wachter
Susan M. Wachter

Preface

In the U.S. and in nearly every other society ever examined, some individuals receive more income and are paid higher wage rates than others. Why? At what cost can society reduce the income differences between the rich and the poor? These are the two main topics in this book.

In a market economy variations in wage rates, which account for most of the differences in income, arise because various skills command different prices and because individuals have different amounts of skills. In this book it is usually assumed that skill prices are fixed. Our answer as to why there are differences in skills is that to a large extent parents are directly or indirectly responsible.

Such a conclusion in some ways differs from the oft expressed idea that the U.S. is an open, highly mobile society in which an individual can succeed if he or she tries hard enough. This conclusion is in greater accord with the more recent idea that poverty may pass in a circle from parent to child.

Nearly all policies that redistribute income also cause a misallocation of resources. The cost of such a misallocation may be large enough to dissuade society from undertaking redistribution. While there are some poorly designed redistribution programs, there are some schemes that are not too costly.

The theoretical and empirical literature on both income distribution and income redistribution are extensive. Rather than trying to cover briefly all possible aspects, I have chosen to concentrate on those topics most closely related to my own research. Unfortunately as a consequence many important areas, for example the role of unions and minimum wages, are not treated at all.

I wish to express my thanks to J. Behrman, Z. Hrubec and T. Wales who co-authored several works which are heavily drawn on in the text.

Thanks also to G. Chamberlain, A. Goldberger, Z. Griliches, S. Jencks, and M. Olneck who have all provided substantial comments and ideas on earlier research but who do not necessarily agree with all the conclusions reached in this book.

Philadelphia, Pennsylvania   P. T.
January 1978

Contents

Introduction 1

If asked to define personal income, most students would probably answer, "The sum of wages, salaries, interest, rents, and dividends." Some might amend this definition by adding transfer payments and, if thinking of disposable personal income, subtracting income taxes. These definitions, in fact, accord reasonably well with the personal or disposable income concepts employed in the National Income Accounts. Economists, however, often use another definition of personal income for any period; namely, the potential amount of goods and services that a person could consume while keeping his wealth or net worth unchanged. The primary practical difference in these two definitions is that the first dwells on transactions in the marketplace, while the second is more comprehensive, including nonmarket activities such as income imputed to owner-occupied houses, the value of self-provided goods and services such as gardening, and capital gains on assets. The two definitions, however, help emphasize the different reasons why economists study and are concerned with the distribution of income.

The first set of questions comes out of the traditional issues connected with the allocation of resources. Such questions would include what determines the market price or wage of different types of labor; what quantity of different types of labor will be offered in the marketplace; and how these prices and quantities will change in response to government policies, new technological discoveries, and growth in the stock of capital. An additional set of questions, whose answers in part depend upon the answers to the earlier ones, are what determines the distribution of income, and why income is not distributed normally but skewed to the right. (These terms are defined in Chapter 2.)

The second definition leads to a set of questions that flow from the observation that the level of goods and services that one consumes or could potentially consume is an important element in a person's standard of living or how well off one is. Thus, economists and others have asked such questions as what percentage of the population live at or below the poverty level,[1] what forces lead to increases or decreases in this percentage, and what policies the government can pursue to reduce poverty.

As the student may have realized, these various questions are related to two different criteria—efficiency and equity—around which much of the discussion of income redistribution revolves. While we will define efficiency more precisely below, roughly it means squeezing the maximum (value of) output out of the economy. Equity, on the other hand, involves fairness or justice, terms that are too important to be defined by economists qua economists but must be left to the dictates of society.

It is worth observing that because of the central position of income in determining well-offness, income is almost unique in being judged by economists and others in terms of both equity and efficiency. Most other issues in resource allocation are judged by economists exclusively in terms of efficiency.

To describe both economic efficiency and equity, a somewhat long digression is in order. Some aspects of this digression are somewhat technical. To facilitate the reader's understanding a more rigorous graphical presentation is given in the appendix to the chapter.

UTILITY MAXIMIZATION

This digression requires the use of two other economic concepts, consumer utility and business production functions which are examined in more detail in the appendix. The basic idea in explaining the behavior of an individual is that the collection of goods purchased should yield the most satisfaction or utility. Individuals can derive utility from many different goods and services. The extra utility obtained from increasing a good or service by one unit (with the quantities of all other goods held constant) is called the marginal utility MU of that good. For most if not all goods and services, the marginal utility received from a good decreases as the quantity consumed of the good grows larger.

An individual with a given income to spend will maximize his or her utility by allocating expenditures such that the marginal utility of the expenditures of the last dollar on each good is the same. That is, suppose there are only two goods, brussels sprouts (X) and steak (Y), whose prices, respec-

---

1 The poverty level is defined in terms of the minimum needs of an individual or family and varies by composition of the family. See Orshansky [1].

tively, are P_X and P_Y. With one dollar the individual could purchase $1/P_X$ or $1/P_Y$ units of X and Y. The individual will maximize his utility when

$$MU_X \left(\frac{1}{P_X}\right) = MU_Y \left(\frac{1}{P_Y}\right) \tag{1}$$

To see that an allocation in which equation (1) holds, yields maximum utility assume on the contrary that the left-hand side of (1) is greater than the right-hand side. Then by reducing expenditures on Y by one unit, the individual has available P_Y dollars which can be used to buy P_Y/P_X units of X. But if the left-hand side of (1) is greater than the right-hand side, then the marginal utility gained from buying P_Y/P_X units of X is greater than the marginal utility lost from giving up one unit of Y, since by rearrangement $MU_X(P_Y/P_X) > MU_Y$. Note that as the individual switches from Y to X, MU_Y will rise and MU_X will fall. With a large enough switch equation, (1) will hold.

PROFIT MAXIMIZATION

Business must decide what to produce and how to produce it. The basic idea in explaining such business choices is profit maximization. Any good is produced by using labor, capital, and other factors of production. The extra output produced by increasing the use of a factor of production by one unit is called the marginal product MP of that factor. It is usually assumed that the MP of a factor decreases as the quantity of the factor used increases with the quantity of all other factors held constant. If there are only two factors—capital, K, and land, L, with prices P_K and P_L used to produce X, then businesses will maximize their profits of X if they use quantities of K and L such that

$$MP_K/P_K = MP_L/P_L \tag{2}$$

The student should be able to prove that equation (2) is the resource allocation that provides the least costly way of producing X or Y by an argument similar to that used for equation (1).

The marginal cost MC of output is the extra cost required to produce one more unit of output. But it follows from equation (2) that the extra cost of producing one more unit of output using labor is $(1/MP_L)$ times P_L. In general for a good X,

$$MC_X = P_K/MP_K = P_L/MP_L \tag{3}$$

As long as MP decreases as more of a factor is used, MC will increase with output produced.

In a competitive economy, the extra revenue received from selling one more unit of X will be P_X. To maximize profits a business should carry the production of X to that point at which its marginal cost equals its price. Similarly, firms should produce that amount of Y where $MC_Y = P_Y$.

EQUILIBRIUM

For an economy an equilibrium position is one in which the allocation of resources will remain unchanged as long as technology and consumer tastes remain fixed. The various conditions given for utility and profit maximization are equilibrium conditions.

FULL EMPLOYMENT

A resource is fully employed if at the price at which transactions are made the units offered by sellers equal the units desired by buyers. In a competitive economy if a resource is not just fully employed, its price will change. The price will fall if purchasers do not want to buy all that is offered, and vice versa.

ECONOMIC EFFICIENCY

Economic efficiency is defined as producing that combination of goods and services which yield the maximum utility to society. Clearly economic efficiency requires full employment, since any unemployed resources could be used to produce goods with positive utility. But economic efficiency requires more. The prices of X and Y enter into the equilibrium conditions of profit and utility maximization. Efficiency requires that the price paid by consumers equals the price received by businesses. If this equality did not hold consumers would be able to improve their utility by reallocating resources, but businesses would find their profits reduced by this reallocation.

Income redistribution affects economic efficiency because the taxes used to finance and the criteria for eligibility for transfer payments cause the prices paid to differ from the prices received. For example, in some current welfare programs, payments are reduced by 50 cents for each dollar earned. To the (potential) worker on welfare the price received is 50% less than the price paid by businesses. This 50% is often referred to as an implicit tax. Income and other explicit taxes levied to finance income redistribution also make P_X paid and received differ.

Both the taxes used to finance the redistribution and the criteria used to distribute the money will generally affect the amount or composition of resources available to society. Income taxes, for example, reduce the rewards from, and cause adjustments in, choices about working in the marketplace, saving, and bearing risks. A reduction in labor and capital will cause fewer material goods to be produced but more leisure time to be enjoyed. Put in another way, policies to redistribute the economic pie as measured by market production also cause the pie to be reduced. In principle, it is possible for the reduction in market output to be so great that everyone in society will have less market consumption after the implementation of the redistributive scheme. Of course, leisure will have increased, but only because the rewards for working are priced and valued too low by the individual. In any event, in judging the appropriateness of the redistribution scheme, society can be concerned with the total size of the national income produced in the marketplace as well as with the distribution of market- and non-market-produced income.

Thus, it is necessary to judge a redistributive scheme on both efficiency and equity terms. Okun calls the conflict between equity and efficiency "the big tradeoff." [2]

EQUITY

As noted at the outset, fairness or justice are not economic concepts and should be defined by society as a whole. A number of different individuals with various political and philosophical bents and a variety of academic and nonacademic backgrounds have written about their image of economic justice. A full discussion of the multitude of ideas is beyond the scope of this book, but a few major ideas must be examined.

One of the major concerns has been about poverty, which is defined more rigorously in Chapter 2, but which essentially involves individuals having an "inadequate" income level. Besides voluminous discussion of what is inadequate, the existing literature can be thought of as defining those who are the "deserving" and the "undeserving" poor. Of course, the former are those society should help; the latter, those society should not help. The terms "deserving" and "undeserving" as applied to the poor, while generally not used, are implicit in eligibility rules for programs such as food stamps and others which transfer resources to individuals.

Transfer programs can be used to redistribute income. But other mechanisms are available. During the 1960s and 1970s, many people have favored programs to increase the skill level and the earnings potential of the poor. Many different programs have been advocated. Some obvious ones are vocational training and increased formal schooling in colleges or prekindergarten. Perhaps less obvious or less remembered now are school lunch and breakfast programs, which in part were advocated to help the child learn more while in classes.

---

2 Okun [2].

The growth in interest in improving the skills of the potentially less able has also led to another debate which can be thought of as the equity, efficiency argument in new clothes. Specifically, some people argue that income redistribution policies should be based on equality of opportunity, while others argue for equality of outcome.

Equality of opportunity is often defined as eliminating all the barriers that prevent individuals from obtaining the training necessary to convert the potential talents implicit in their genetic endowments into capabilities. Such barriers would include discrimination, poor nutrition, or unequal access to loans to finance education.

Advocates of equality of outcome argue that even if all barriers to equality in training were removed, the resulting distribution of income would be too inequitable; hence, it is appropriate and necessary to undertake the policies to redistribute income—perhaps to the point of everyone having the same after-tax income.

Some equality of opportunity programs do not cause losses in economic efficiency. For example, it can be shown that racial discrimination results in some blacks and some whites ending up in occupations for which they are not best suited and, average income for blacks to be less than for equally qualified whites. Eliminating discrimination will improve efficiency and redistribute income between the two groups. It may also cause both blacks and whites to have higher incomes. But generally, equality of outcome requires policies that involve a tradeoff between equity and efficiency.

In the remainder of this book, we examine the degree of inequality in the distribution of income and how inequality has changed over time. We investigate the sources of inequality within and between generations in personal earnings, information which is relevant to the author's concept of fairness and to certain policy issues. We then examine the efficiency aspects of various redistribution schemes. The book concludes with some thoughts on the need for redistribution and a better system to accomplish redistribution.

REFERENCES

1. Mollie Orshansky. "Counting the Poor." *Social Security Bulletin* 28: 3-29 (1965).

2. Arthur M. Okun. *Equality and Efficiency: The Big Tradeoff.* Washington, D. C.: Brookings Institution, 1975.

Appendix to
Chapter 1

This appendix contains a graphical presentation of utility functions and indifference curves. It will also derive the production possibility frontier which will be used to present the economic efficiency concept in a more rigorous way.

Suppose the only two goods in the economy are brussels sprouts and beefsteak. A utility function describes how well off an individual feels for any particular combination of sprouts and steak. A useful device in utility analysis is the idea of an indifference curve, which indicates all the combinations of sprouts and steak which leave an individual feeling equally well off. For example, in Figure 1.1 the combination shown at M places the individual on the indifference curve labeled I. However, because the individual obtains satisfaction from both goods, he could trade some sprouts for some steak and have the same level of utility. For example, increasing sprouts and decreasing steak till the point R was reached would still leave this person on indifference curve I. The shape of the indifference curve, incidentally, is MU_X/MU_Y (where X and Y are, respectively, sprouts and steak), since it is necessary for the loss in utility from reducing Y equal the gain in utility from increasing X for the individual to be indifferent.

In this figure there is another indifference curve labeled II. Consider the point $R*$ on II. At $R*$ the individual has more steak and the same amount of sprouts as at R on indifference curve I. Therefore, as long as the additional steak has positive utility, the individual must have more utility at $R*$ than at R. But since the individual is indifferent between $R*$ and any other point on II and is indifferent between R and any other point on I, indifference curve II, which lies above and to the right of I, must represent more utility than curve I. This same type of argument can be used to show that it is impossible for an individual's indifference curves to intersect.

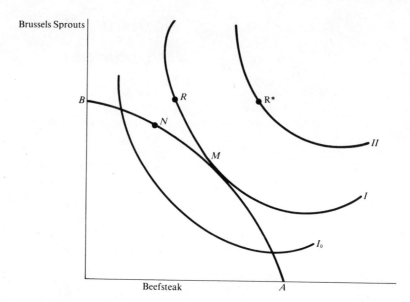

Fig. 1.1 Indifference Curves and Production Possibility Curves.

A production function indicates how various combinations of factor inputs such as capital and labor can be combined to produce output. When there are only two inputs, K and L, it is easy to portray graphically equal production curves (or isoquants), which indicate the various combinations of K and L which produce a given level of output of one good. Since we will not use such curves later in this book, they are not shown here, but they look like the indifference curves in Fig. 1.1. The shape of such equal production curves is given by the ratio, MP_K/MP_L.

Society can use capital and labor to produce both steak and brussels sprouts. The production possibility frontier indicates the various combinations of output of sprouts and steak than can be achieved if all resources are fully employed. As resources are transferred from the production of sprouts, more steak can be produced. For example, it may be possible to produce 100 pecks of brussels sprouts or 25 pounds of beef. Alternatively, it may be possible to produce 65 pecks of sprouts and 70 pounds of beef. The production possibility frontier is drawn as AB in Fig. 1.1.

Economic efficiency is defined as producing that set of goods and services which yield the maximum utility. If in our society every consumer had the same utility function, the economywide indifference curve would be the same as that drawn for the individual in Fig. 1. Then in Fig. 1.1, M would represent a point where the economy was operating at maximum efficiency. That is, any diversion of resources to the production of more or less brussels sprouts would lead to a reduction in utility. In terms of the figure, any other point on *AB* would only allow society to reach an indifference curve that lies below and to the left of *I* such as I_0, which intersects *AB*. In Fig. 1, the maximum utility is achieved when the production possibility frontier is tangent to an indifference curve.

Now, suppose everyone were identical to individual 2. A different combination of sprouts and steak would yield the maximum utility. Since individual 2 likes sprouts more than individual 1 does, the tangency of the new indifference curve (which is not shown to avoid clutter) would occur at a point such as *N*. This point is also economically efficient.

Both points *M* and *N* were obtained by assuming that everyone had No. 1's or No. 2's taste. When different people have different tastes, it is still possible to develop an economywide average utility function and indifference curve. Such an average indifference curve would be tangent to *AB* between points *M* and *N*. Ignoring for a moment certain complications, redistribution of income between No. 1 and No. 2 would cause the economy to shift to a new efficient point along *AB*. Society, in this instance, could judge the proposed redistribution solely in terms of fairness or equity.

Redistribution schemes, however, will generally cause individuals to alter the amount of labor they will supply to the marketplace. Thus, redistribution will shift the production possibility frontier for marketplace goods and services inward; for example, from *AB* to *CD* in Fig. 1.2. Some indifference curve will be tangent to *CD* at a point such as *T* which will be the new equilibrium point. On the *CD* production possibility frontier, it is not possible to have as much of both steak and sprouts as along *AB*; hence, the new equilibrium must have less of at least one of the goods, though having more leisure.

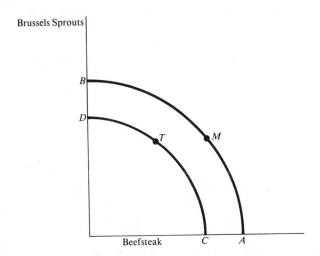

Fig. 1.2 Two Production Possibility Frontiers.

Fig. 1.2 ignores what happens to leisure. In Chapter 7 it is shown that if leisure is included in the analysis, redistribution schemes will result in an equilibrium in which the indifference curve intersects AB. As explained above, it is the indifference curve which is tangent to AB which provides the most welfare. Thus, to achieve more equity there will be a loss in economic efficiency.

Inequality in 2
Personal Income

In this chapter we will examine some of the important features of the distribution of annual personal income at a point of time and consider how the inequality has changed during this century. Much of the analysis in this chapter focuses on the distribution of *family income*, which is believed to be the concept most closely related to the concept of distribution of economic welfare.[1] However, much of the subsequent analysis will be concerned with individual earnings. The switch is made partly because most economic theory deals with individual's earning capacity and partly because subjects such as who marries whom and the labor-force participation of wives is beyond the scope of this book.

1. The Distribution of Family Personal Income

Figure 2.1 contains two frequency distributions. The first, *AA*, is the so-called normal curve which is symmetrical and bell-shaped. The second, *BB*, is not symmetrical, since for example a majority of the people have a less than average income. The averages of the two distributions are the same because more people in *BB* have very high incomes. The actual distribution of income in this country and in most other countries is similar to the *BB* curve.[2] Indeed, the *BB* curve represents the distribution of family personal income in 1971.

---

1 Some economists would argue that family per capita income is even more appropriate, but the distribution of such a measure is available only for recent years. See Morgan et al. [1].

2 One particular theoretical distribution that is shaped like the *BB* curve is the lognormal. However, detailed studies have generally concluded that the observed distribution is not exactly lognormal.

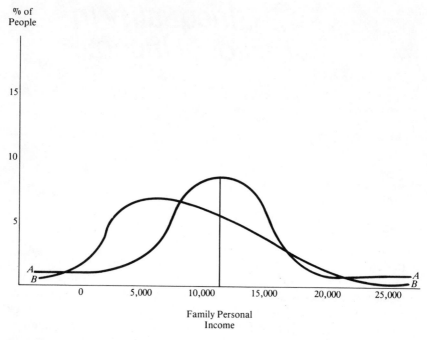

Fig. 2.1 Two Hypothetical Distributions of Income.

Family personal income is defined as the sum of wage and salary income, property income (except corporate retained earnings), and nonmoney income. The breakdown of family personal income is given in Table 2.1 for both 1964 and 1971.

As shown in this table, about 70% of personal income occurs in the form of wages and salaries, even excluding the wage component in self-employment income and royalties. Self-employment, property, and money transfer income (a somewhat mislabeled category, as explained below) each accounts for about 9% of family personal income. Imputed income accounts for 5%, while Medicare benefits and food stamps, which are nonmoney transfer payments, account for no more than 1¼% of family personal income.[3] At first glance, this table suggests remarkable stability in the sources of personal income over a seven-year period. There are, however, some important shifts. For example, the growth in both types of transfer income, and especially of the sum of Medicare benefits and food stamps from

---

3 Imputed income represents income that would be received if an asset were rented in the marketplace instead of being used by the owner. The major component is for owner-occupied housing.

Table 2.1 Composition of Family Personal Income by Type, Percentage of Family Personal Income

		1964	1971
1.	Family Personal Income	100.0%	100.0%
2.	Wage and Salary	69.1	69.4
3.	Self-employment	10.7	8.4
4.	Property Income [a]	9.3	9.2
5.	Money Transfer Income	8.5	10.8
6.	Total Money Income	97.6	97.8
7.	Imputed Income	5.1	4.8
8.	Medicare Benefits	0.0	1.0
9.	Net Value of Food Stamps	0.0	0.2
10.	Total Non-Monetary Income	5.1	6.0
11.	Minus Contribution for Social Insurance [b]	2.6	3.8

Source: *Survey of Current Business* (October 1974), p. 20

[a] Does not include either capital-gains income or corporate retained earnings.

[b] Personal contributions to social security are deducted because transfer payments include social security benefits.

0% to 1.2% is notable. Also, there is a decline in self-employment income— a trend which is even more noticeable over longer periods of time.

Fig. 2.1 clearly indicates differences in the level of income received by various families. Some of this variation can be attributed to the characteristics of the family or its members, such as the age or the education of the head of the family. For example, in Table 2.2 it can be seen that average family personal income rises concurrently with the education level of the head of the family. Family personal income increases with the age of the head of the family until the 45 to 54-year-old group is reached, and then income begins to decline. Additionally, income is greater for whites than for nonwhites. In subsequent chapters, we will examine in more detail the theoretical and empirical relationships between income or labor earnings and these characteristics. At this point, we will turn to the discussion of the measurement and meaning of inequality.

2. Inequality

While the income distribution is often described by the frequency curves given in Fig. 2.1, inequality is generally measured with other devices. Two such interrelated devices are the Lorenz curve and the distribution of income shares. It is always possible to rank individuals or families in a population in order of their income. It is also easy to calculate the total income in

Table 2.2 Average (1964) family personal income by characteristics of head

Type of consumer unit	Average family personal income Thousands of $
Age	
14 − 24	$4.7
25 − 34	7.3
35 − 44	9.2
45 − 54	9.6
55 − 64	8.3
65 and over	5.8
Education	
Elementary only	5.6
High School (not completed)	7.0
High School (completed)	8.3
College less than 4 years	9.4
College 4 years	12.4
Graduate School	13.4
Color	
White	8.2
Nonwhite	4.7

Source: *Survey of Current Business* (October 1974), p. 28.

the population and the share of this total received by any group such as those who rank from the bottom to the 20th percentile. (This group will often be referred to as the bottom fifth.)

We will examine first the family personal income received by families and by consumer units in the United States in several different years. Here, a family is defined as two or more persons living together and related by blood or marriage. Consumer units are families, as just defined, and unrelated individuals.

Earlier, we observed that one useful way of describing inequality is the share of total income received by various groups as defined by their position in the income distribution chart. Table 2.3 contains these shares for various years for each of the five fifths. Consider first the distribution in 1971. In that year, the poorest fifth of all consumer units received nearly 5% of the total personal income, and the richest fifth received nearly 45% of the total income. For families, the poorest and richest fifths received 6½% and 42% of total personal income, respectively. Since the terms "poorest" and "richest" by themselves tend to conjure up images of starving children and unbridled luxury, it is worth noting that in 1971 when prices were about

Table 2.3 Distribution of family personal income by income fifths—1964, 1971

Fifth	1964 All Consumer Units	Families	1971 All Consumer Units	Families
Bottom	4.2%	5.8%	4.8%	6.6%
Second	10.6	11.8	10.8	12.1
Third	16.4	16.7	16.4	16.8
Fourth	23.2	22.5	23.3	22.5
Top	45.5	43.1	44.6	42.0

40% lower than they are now, the *average* income of families in the United States was $11,500 while the *average* income in the lowest and highest fifths was $2,800 and $25,700, respectively. A discussion of whether or not families with an income of $2,800 are starving will be postponed to section 2.4 on poverty.

In 1964 the shares received by each fifth were similar to those in 1971, but there was a small increase in the share received by each of the lowest two fifths and a decrease in the share of the top fifth. This is often described as a decrease in inequality (a more rigorous definition is given below). Most of this decline was concentrated in the top 5%, whose share was 18.8% in 1964 and 17.8% in 1971. Detailed calculations indicate that the increase in the share of the bottom fifth is due to the increase in transfer payments, as shown in Table 2.1. Indeed, there is some indication that the distribution of income exclusive of transfer payments became more unequally distributed during this time period.

A closely related, but at times more informative, description of inequality is provided by the Lorenz curve. On the vertical axis of this curve is represented the (cumulative) percent of income received by the lowest x% of families, and on the horizontal axis is represented the cumulative percentage of income-receiving units. The resulting curve will tell us that in 1971 the bottom 20% (or bottom fifth) of families received 6.6% of income, while the lowest 40% (or lowest two fifths) received 18.7% of income. This information is also given in Table 2.3. But the Lorenz curve for 1971, given as the curved line in Fig. 2.2, contains this information for all income rankings or groupings.

In addition to this greater detail, the Lorenz curve helps us to better understand certain problems. In order to see this, consider what the distribution would be if everyone had the same income. Then, the lowest 10% of recipients would receive 10% of the total income, the lowest 20% of recipients

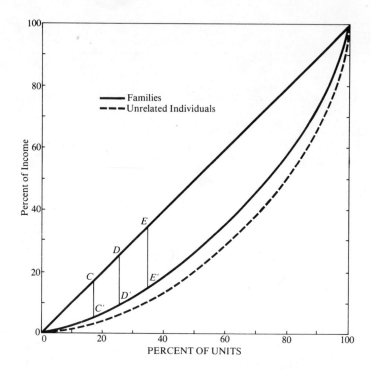

Fig. 2.2 Family Personal Income, 1971. (*Source:* U.s. Department of Commerce. Bureau of Economic Analysis, *Survey of Current Business* (October 1974), p. 19.)

would receive 20% of the total income, and so on. This hypothetically completely equal distribution would then result in the straight diagonal line, AA, connecting the corners of the figure.

One often used quantitative measure of inequality is the area between the diagonal curve and the Lorenz curve. This area is proportional to the Gini coefficient, a typical value of which for the United States is about 0.4. If there is no inequality of income, the Gini coefficient will be zero. On the other hand, if one family had all the income in society, the Gini coefficient would be 1. Consider for the moment the implications of this measured area. The area between any two Lorenz curves can be calculated by adding together their vertical differences at all income levels—that is, by adding the distance *CC'* to *DD'* to *EE'*, etc. Now examine Fig. 2.3, which contains several Lorenz curves. Curves *I* and *II* intersect one another twice. Thus, according to curve *II*, the middle classes have a smaller share of income, while the upper and lower classes have larger shares of income. It is possible for the area between the diagonal and curve *I* to be greater than, equal to, or less than the area between the diagonal and curve *II*. Suppose the two dis-

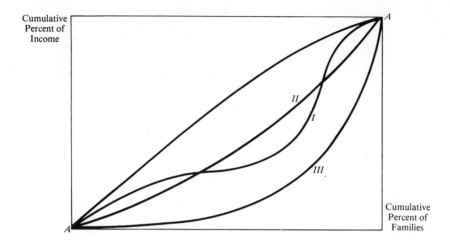

Fig. 2.3 Three Hypothetical Lorenz Curves.

tances are equal. There has been a redistribution of income, but the area measure says that there is no change in equality. This apparent contradiction occurs because the area measure gives equal weight to all distances between the Lorenz curves and the diagonal regardless of the level of income. If these distances are given different weights, it would be possible to conclude that between curve *I* and curve *II* inequality has increased or decreased. Indeed, it has been shown that in the absence of the knowledge of how to weight these distances it is only possible to state unambiguously that inequality has decreased if one Lorenz curve never intersects but always lies inside another. For example, both curves *I* and *II* in Fig. 2.3 lie within curve *III*.

The Lorenz curves for 1929, 1964, and 1971 are given in Fig. 2.4. None of these curves intersects, and inequality has apparently decreased greatly from 1929 to 1964 and slightly thereafter. (Thus, the previous statement about decreases in inequality based on the shares happens to be correct, since the Lorenz curves for 1964 and 1971 do not intersect.)

3. Trends in Inequality

In the previous section we examined changes in the shares of family personal income on the Lorenz curve between 1964 and 1971. We concluded that there appeared to be a slight shift between 1964 and 1971 and a larger shift between 1929 and 1964. In this section we will examine this question in more detail and indicate why the term "appeared" was used.

Table 2.4 contains the shares of family personal income received by the various fifths of all consumer units as well as the shares of the top 5% in se-

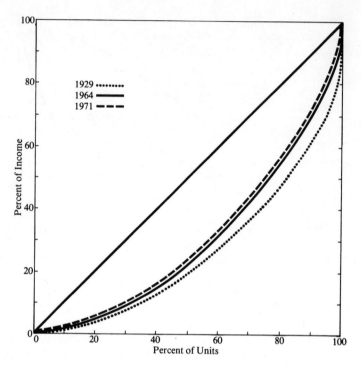

Fig. 2.4 Lorenz Curves of Family Personal Income of Consumer Units, 1929, 1964, 1971. (*Source:* U.S. Department of Commerce, Bureau of Economic Analysis, *Survey of Current Business* (October 1974), p. 20.)

Table 2.4 Distribution of family personal income, all consumer units, selected years

	Old series [a]				New Series [a]		
	1929	*1941*	*1944*	*1950*	*1961*	*1964*	*1971*
Fifths							
Lowest	3.5%	4.1%	4.9%	4.8%	4.6%	4.2%	4.8
Second	9.0	9.5	10.9	10.9	10.9	10.6	10.8
Third	13.8	15.3	16.2	16.1	16.3	16.4	16.4
Fourth	19.3	22.3	22.2	22.1	22.7	23.2	23.3
Fifth	54.4	48.8	45.8	46.1	45.5	45.5	44.6
Top 5%	30.0	24.0	20.7	21.4	19.6	20.0	19.1

Source: *Survey of Current Business* (October 1974), p. 27.
[a] The two series are not completely comparable.

lected years between 1929 and 1971.[4] Taken at face value, the data in this table suggest a substantial decrease in inequality between 1929 and 1941. A further decrease in inequality was observed by 1944, and only slight decreases in inequality were subsequently recorded. For example, the share of the richest fifth was 54.4% in 1929, 45.8% in 1944, and 44.6% in 1971.

While there are some data on the distribution of income by fifth prior to 1929, most economists do not trust them.[5] Data collected by Kuznets suggest that the share of the top 1% and 5% exhibits no trend between 1913 and 1930. See [2], p. 19.

The data shown in Table 2.4, however, may be masking some important shifts in inequality because some marked changes have occurred during the period under consideration in the composition of the population, in consumer units, and in the concept of income. One of the most important and complex elements here is connected with the age distribution. If the reader refers to Table 2.2, he will note that income varies with the age of the head of the family. The age distribution of heads of families or consumer units has varied over time because of the fluctuations in birth rate (e.g., very low in the 1930s but very high in the late 1940s) and the lengthening of the life span coupled with the growing proportion of the population which is retired from employment. If we were to examine the inequality of lifetime income, the fluctuations in the age composition would not be important, but when (as in Table 2.4) we study annual income, inequality will be increased when there is a larger proportion of those under 24 or over 65 whose average income is far less than the average in the whole population. In addition, inequality tends to vary with age. For example, Taubman [3] has calculated Lorenz curves for annual earnings for 1955 and 1969 for a particular group of men who were about 33 and 47 years old in the two periods. In this sample the Lorenz curve for 1955 was inside that for 1969. Mincer [4] also presents data that the inequality of annual earnings varies with age. Thus, changes in the age composition between the various years could affect the trends in inequality.

The problems caused by shifts in the age distribution are even more considerable because of related shifts in family composition. Much earlier in the century, it would not be uncommon for elderly parents to live with their children or for new entrants to the labor force to live with their parents. The income position of all members in such a family would be judged by their combined income. Now many retired persons do not live with their children, and many new labor-force entrants leave the nest for an apartment.

---

4 The data are labeled old and new series because of substantial changes in methodology which may affect comparability over time. See the article cited for a discussion.

5 See Miller [2] (p. 27, note 6) for a discussion of this point.

To some extent, these uncouplings represent voluntary choices which would presumably indicate that the individuals involved are more satisfied to live apart than to live together. But, the elderly couple with social security benefits of, say, $3,000 in 1971 or $4,000 in 1974 would be placed in the lowest income fifth—even if they have higher consumption financed by previous savings.

Another potentially important problem with the interpretation of the data in Table 2.4 is the changing role of women. A much greater proportion of women work today than did 20 or 40 years ago, and much of this increase is among married women. For example, the proportion of married women in the labor force has risen from 16% in 1940 to about 50% today. Family income includes the income of all of the members of the family. The effect of women's earnings on trends in family income inequality, therefore, depends upon changes in the income level of the woman's spouse. There is some indication that in the past women were more likely to work if their husbands either were temporarily unemployed or generally had low incomes. Thus, women tended to equalize the distribution of *measured* family income. It is not obvious, at the time of this writing, whether the trend in labor-force participation has led to greater or lesser equality over time, though there is a suspicion that more women whose husbands' income would have placed them in upper- and middle-family income levels are now working and thus increasing inequality in *measured* family income. "Measured" has been emphasized in the previous sentences because housework is real work even if it is not include in the statistics on family income. Some of the increased labor-force participation of women has been accompanied by a decrease in housework, as for example, by the use of more convenience foods. Thus, money income may not be a stable index over time of economic welfare.

A third major problem with the interpretation of the data in Table 2.4 is the measure of income used. In addition to the exclusion of household labor from calculations of family income (as described above), corporate retained earnings and capital gains are not included in the income measure. The corporate form of business has become more important as the self-employed sector has declined and corporate retained earnings have become significant—amounting to about 10% of personal income in the economy as a whole now (it was much less in 1929). People in the top fifth of the income distribution own most of the stock of those corporations with large amounts of retained earnings.

Additionally, because of tax laws, corporations increasingly have tended to pay their top executives with items such as stock options which yield capital gains and with other schemes which defer compensation to the time the executive retires and is in a lower tax bracket. These items are generally not included in wage-and-salary or current income figures. Data in Lewellyn [5] suggest that these tax-induced changes may be very important—accounting for nearly half of the after-tax compensation of top corporate executives in recent years—and have probably caused a noticeable understatement of the share of total income going to the top 5%. For example, he has calculated that in 1963 if the top executives had received their compensation solely in the form of salaries, their before-tax salaries would have to be 10 times as large as their actual compensation in all forms for these executives to receive their current after-tax income.

Another difficulty with the data in Table 2.4 is that they refer to annual income. In judging economic welfare we are interested in the distribution of the present discounted value of lifetime income, since families can save and borrow to smooth out some of both the systematic variation with age shown in Table 2.2 or the annual random fluctuation in income.

Recently several samples which follow the same people over time have been analyzed for stability of the distribution of annual earnings. Taubman [3] ranks individuals in the NBER-TH sample by their earnings in 1955. He then examines both the relative position of the men in their 1969 earnings distribution and their growth rate in earnings between 1955 and 1969. In terms of earnings position he finds "regression towards the mean," with those below average in 1955 tending to move up and those above the mean tending to move down. However, except for those in the top and bottom tenths of the 1955 distribution, the particular tenths that presumably contain a disproportionate number of people with (for them) unusually high and low annual earnings, the average growth rate was the same regardless of earnings level in 1955.

Lillard and Willis [6] in a recent paper that uses seven continuous years of earnings in the Michigan Income Dynamic Sample have estimated that roughly 75% of the individual variation in annual earnings is variation in permanent or lifetime earnings. However, they only study earnings for non-retirees. Since Table 2.2 contains retirees and is for income rather than earnings, a larger proportion of the inequality is not permanent. Still, it seems likely that the variation in the permanent part of income is about 70% of the variation in annual income. Moreover, there is little reason to suspect that the trends of inequality in permanent or lifetime income are different from those in annual income except for the reasons discussed above.

These and other problems with the data suggest that it is difficult to be certain that there has been a marked decline in inequality in annual or lifetime income from 1929 to the present without making the proper adjustments. Some of these adjustments are easy to effect. For example, suppose that in two time periods those who were 65 and over increased from 5% to 10%. It is possible to calculate what the inequality would be in the second period if the elderly were still 5% by discarding a random half of the observations on the elderly. Essentially, this amounts to reweighting the observations to correspond to the weights in a given year. Most studies which have looked at inequality before and after such reweighting have found no change in the trend of inequality, though Smith and Welch [8] and Paglin [9], discussed below, find that the changing age distribution has tended to offset some decrease in inequality between 1960 and 1970, or over the postwar period. However, such reweighting schemes do not address themselves to the question of whether today's elderly are like those of 50 years ago or whether having more young and more old people in separate families with relatively low income has affected the trend.

Paglin [9] has proposed an adjustment to the usual Lorenz curve approach which partly corrects for the changing age distribution in another way. As shown in Table 2.2, average earnings varies with age. When the population of people who are young or old increases, more people will be further from the average earnings in the population. Paglin, in effect, proposes to compare the actual Lorenz curve for a person of a given age with the equal annual-income line for people of the same age. He then adds up the results for the different age groups. For the postwar period, Paglin calculates that such an adjustment would raise the share going to the bottom fifth by at least 25%, e.g., from 5% to 6¼%, and that the distribution has grown more equal over time. He has not, however, adjusted for uncoupling of families, nor for certain interrelationships between annual and lifetime earnings explained in Chapter 3.

It is not clear if the necessary adjustments to account fully for changing age distribution, labor-force participation, and income concepts have caused the trend in inequality to be understated or overstated. With no clear guide as to whether the trend is or is not overstated, most economists argue that numbers in Table 2.4 are indicative of the trends or, in other words, that inequality in lifetime income before tax lessened after 1929, but has remained roughly constant since the end of World War II.

4. The Poverty Population

Many people are concerned with the distribution of income because of its relationship to poverty. Poverty can be defined in many ways. The so-called official poverty level is defined as follows. The Bureau of Labor Statistics annually collects data on the amount of income needed to maintain a "high," an "intermediate," and a "low" standard of living for families of various sizes in different geographical regions. The food proportion of the low standard is reduced to one-sixth of its actual level, which represents the emergency level that the government states a family should subsist on for only a short period of time. The poverty level is then set at three times the emergency food level. For an urban family of four, the poverty level was about $3,000 in 1968 and $5,000 in 1974. Assuming consumption of three meals a day, those urban families of four exactly at the poverty level are calculated to spend less than 40 cents per meal per person.

Since the poverty level varies by family size and geographic location, it is not possible to go directly from information on the share of income held by the bottom fifth to the percentage of the population living at or below the poverty level. However, the government does estimate this percentage from more detailed data. As shown in Fig. 2.5, the percentage of the population living in poverty (the incidence rate) has declined from about 33% of the population in the late 1940s to about 11½% today. The student will note that the downward trend has not been smooth. The year-to-year increases in the incidence of poverty (e.g., from 1973 to 1974) correspond to periods of increasing unemployment. The primary reason for the changes in the incidence of poverty is changes in gross national product per capita.

Poverty does not fall equally on all groups in the United States. Table 2.5 contains information on the makeup of the poverty population in 1974. Of the 24 million people in the poverty group, 14% are at least 65 years old. The elderly poor constituted about 16% of the elderly. About 78 of those in the poverty group live in families, with roughly two-thirds of these headed by whites. Of the nonelderly families, slightly more than half are headed by a male. Thus, poverty is not exclusively the domain of the blacks or of female-headed families.

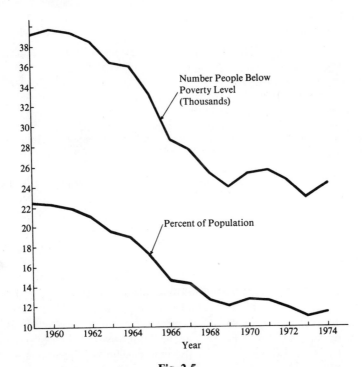

Fig. 2.5

Source: U. S. Bureau of the Census, Current Population Reports Series, p 60.

Table 2.5 Poverty distribution of people in 1974

Characteristic of head	Number of people in millions	Percentage of poverty group	Percentage of own group in population
Total People	24.2	100%	11.6
People 65 and Over	3.3	14	16
Unrelated Individuals	2.1	9	32
Family, Head 65 and Over	.8	3	10
Head Under 65	2.6	89	11
Unrelated Individuals	2.8	12	23
White	2.0	8	20
Male-headed	.9	4	16
Female-headed	1.1	5	22
Non-white	.6	3	33
Male-headed	.3	1	33
Female-headed	.4	2	58
Families	18.8	78	10
White	12.0	50	8
Male-headed	7.8	32	5
Female-headed	4.2	17	33
Non-white	6.8	28	28
Male-headed	2.4	10	13
Female-headed	4.2	18	56

Note: Some people over 65 live in households headed by persons under 65. The categories "Head 65 and over" and "unrelated individuals over 65" do not add to total people over 65 in the poverty class since some elderly live with their children.

Whites and male-headed families generate so many people in the poverty group because they are a large proportion of the population. When viewed in terms of what percentage of a particular population group are in the poverty group, a different picture emerges. For example, more than one half of nonwhite female-headed families and individuals but only 5% of white-male-headed families are in this group.

A term such as "poverty" implies substantial hardship, as is underscored by the calculation that the individuals in this group in 1974 spent less than 40 cents per meal. However, the social significance of low income would be reduced if those in the poverty group in one year have much higher incomes in most other years. The breakdown of the poverty group in Table 2.5 reveals groups such as the elderly who receive a steady, low income. Moreover, studies such as those of Lillard and Willis [6] and Diamond et al. [7] indicate that most people who receive low earnings in one year remain in the bottom of the distribution for many years.

Concentrations of poverty in particular groups can affect the feasibility of various programs designed to reduce poverty. Employment programs for female-headed households, for example, may work only if day-care centers are set up for children, and even then the children may suffer from not being with a parent during the day.

5. Taxes and Government Expenditures

Our discussion of the distribution of income has been based on pretax family income defined as labor income plus dividends, interest, and other returns on financial investment, plus transfer payments. We are interested in the distribution of income as a measure of ability to consume goods and services, and we have discussed some of the limitations of these data as such a measure. Taxes and government expenditures provide, however, one important limitation we have not yet discussed. Taxes are collected to pay for both the goods and the services purchased by the government on behalf of its citizens and income redistribution programs. Since many such redistribution programs have already been included in the family income measure, it is appropriate that we deduct the taxes to finance them from the incomes of the payees.[6] However, most transfer programs are not paid for by special taxes but are financed from proceeds from income and other taxes. These general revenues are also collected to pay for defense and other goods and services. These goods and services provide benefits to consumers, and in principle it would be possible to allocate some of these benefits to families with particular levels of income. With such an allocation, it would be possible to calculate the shares by fifth in after-tax income plus government expenditures. But while it may be possible to allocate expenditures on health clinics reasonably accurately, major items in the budget such as for defense, for the president, and for Congress and the courts present unsolvable difficulties. Therefore, we shall first examine the distribution of after-tax income and then the distribution including arbitrarily allocated government expenditures.

One of the major difficulties in examining the effects of taxes is deciding who "bears the burden" or what the "incidence" of a tax is. Do corporations, for example, suffer a reduction in their after-tax rate of return when the corporate income tax rate is raised? This and related questions are still unsolved. However, these questions are not relevant for deciding what is the current amount of inequality, since any tax-induced changes in behav-

---

6 The redistributive programs included in the family income series are all those involving cash and some of those involving goods and services. Other services such as health clinics have not been included.

ior by, say, corporations that increase their before-tax profits to offset a tax increase are already included in the existing before-tax income-distribution data.

Recently Okner [10] has calculated the effective tax rate—taxes paid divided by pretax income including transfers and unrealized capital gains. Since he is also interested in who bears the burden of the tax, he makes a number of alternative assumptions. However, for our purpose we merely wish to examine the existing after-tax distribution which is approximated by his "most progressive" variant. The results for 1966 and 1970 for this variant are given in Fig. 2.6a and 2.6b.

Except for people at the very lowest end of the scale, the effective tax rate increases gradually with income throughout the income range. The drop in the effective rate at the very low end occurs for several reasons. First, people with temporarily very low incomes consume more than their current income and pay sales taxes on part of this consumption. Second, many retirees have property income or real estate which are often taxed heavily. In judging these high tax rates on low income the reader should recall that most transfer payments also go to families with low incomes. For both 1966 and 1970, Okner calculates that the area between the Lorenz curve and the equal distribution line is about 5% smaller after taxes than before taxes but with transfer income included in the before-tax figures.

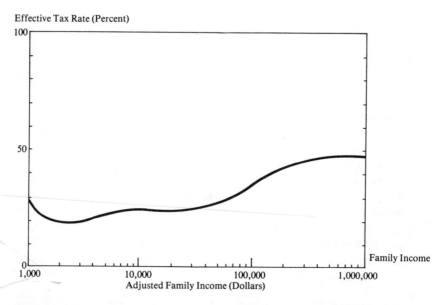

Fig. 2.6a Effective Rates of Federal, State, and Local Taxes, 1966. (*Source:* Okner, "Total U. s. Tax Burdens: 1966 and 1970 Compared.")

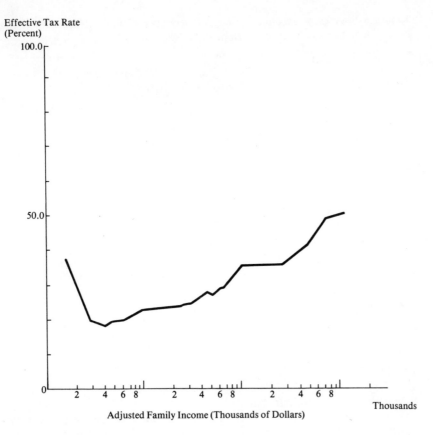

Fig. 2.6b Effective Rates of Federal, State, and Local Taxes. (*Source:* Okner, ibid.)

This movement would be greater if a comparison were made between pretax family income excluding transfer payments and post-tax family income including transfers.

Reynolds and Smolensky [11] have calculated the effects of taxes, transfers, and government expenditures on the distribution of income. Using assumptions similar to Okner on taxes, allocating transfers and specific expenditures such as health clinics by the income of the recipient or users, and general expenditures by income and by population, they calculate the Gini coefficient, which is proportional to the area between the Lorenz curve and the equal distribution line, has declined in three selected post-World War II years. As shown in Table 2.6 the Gini coefficient declined by around 70 to 100 points or 15% to 25% in each of the three years. Taxes, transfers, and expenditures all lead to more equality. It is notable how much more important transfers and less important are taxes are in 1970.

Table 2.6 Sources of absolute declines in inequality (Gini Coefficient times 100). Normal incidence, 1950, 1961, 1970, Factor NNP

	1950	*Gini x 1000* *1961*	*1970*
Change in Gini From			
1. General Government	20	36	36
2. Taxes	10	5	−8 [a]
a) Personal Income	15	15	8
b) Social Security	−4 [a]	−2 [a]	−6 [a]
c) Corporation Income	4	3	2
d) Property Tax	−3 [a]	−5 [a]	−7 [a]
e) Other [b]	−4 [a]	−6 [a]	−5 [a]
3. Transfer Payments	25	36	53
a) Social Security	8	20	34
b) Other [c]	16	17	20
4. Other Specific Expenditures	16	18	26
a) Federal [d]	13	7	9
b) State & Local [e]	2	10	17
5. Total Decline Gini Coefficient	73	95	106

Source: Reynolds and Smolensky [11].

[a] Negative sign indicates that the item raises rather than lowers the post-fisc Gini coefficient relative to initial inequality.

[b] Sales, Excises and Customs, Estate and Gift Taxes.

[c] Public Assistance, Other Welfare, Unemployment Compensation, and Other Transfers.

[d] Veterans' benefits; Net interest paid; Agriculture; Elementary, Secondary, and Other Education; Higher Education; Highways; Labor; and Housing and Community Development.

[e] Veterans' benefits, Net interest paid, Agriculture, Elementary, Secondary and Other Education; Higher Education, Highways and Labor.

They also present data on the initial and postgovernment (or post-fisc) distribution by shares for people in various fifths. As shown in Table 2.7, there is a big increase post-fisc in the share of all but the top fifth. Reynolds and Smolensky's particular results are sensitive to assumptions made, but they report that all alternative assumptions support the view that the post-fisc distribution is much more equally distributed than the before-tax income distribution. It is not obvious, however, if there is a trend in this mea-

Table 2.7 Predicted share of income, quintiles, 1950, 1961, and 1970

Percentile share	Factor income [a]			Standard post-fisc [b]			Standard post-fisc w/o GE [c]		
	1950	*1961*	*1970*	*1950*	*1961*	*1970*	*1950*	*1961*	*1970*
Share of Lowest 20%	3.6%	3.3%	2.9%	6.4%	6.4%	6.7%	5.6%	5.2%	5.4%
Share of Middle 60%	48.5	47.7	46.5	53.7	53.8	54.2	52.6	51.9	52.2
Share of Highest 20%	48.0	49.0	50.6	39.9	39.8	39.1	41.8	42.9	42.4
Share of Highest 5%	14.7	15.1	15.8	11.6	11.5	11.2	12.3	12.7	12.5

Source: Reynolds and Smolensky [11].

[a] Before-tax and transfer income.
[b] Factor income adjusted for taxes, transfers, and government expenditures.
[c] Factor income adjusted for taxes and transfers.

sure of inequality. Unfortunately, comparable data prior to 1940 are not available.

6. Conclusion

In this chapter we have examined the shape of the distribution of family personal income, the extent of inequality in income, and the incidence of poverty and the trends in the later two categories. We have seen that there are some systematic and regular features to the shape. There is also some indication of a decrease in inequality and in the incidence of poverty—subject to some important qualifications.

In subsequent chapters we shall try to explain why the income distribution has its particular characteristics and why there is inequality. Most of the relevant theory, however, applies to the earnings of individuals rather than to family income. Thus, individual earnings will become the focus of our analysis. Fortunately, most of the descriptions of inequality and related trends employed in this chapter on family income apply equally well to individual earnings—which is not too surprising, since wages and salaries amount to 70% of personal income.

REFERENCES

1. James Morgan et al. *Five Thousand American Families—Patterns of Economic Progress*, vol. 1. Ann Arbor: Institute for Social Research, 1974.

2. Herman P. Miller. *Income Distribution in the United States*. Washington, D. C.: Government Printing Office, 1966.

3. Paul Taubman. *Sources of Inequality of Earnings*. Amsterdam: North Holland, 1975.

4. Jacob Mincer. *Schooling, Experience, and Earnings*. New York: National Bureau of Economic Research, 1974.

5. William Lewellen. *Executive Compensation in Large Industrial Corporations*. New York: Columbia University Press, 1968.

6. Lee A. Lillard and Robert J. Willis. "Dynamic Aspects of Earnings Mobility." *Econometrica*, forthcoming.

7. Peter Diamond et al. Appendix B in *Report of the Consultant Panel on Social Security to the Congressional Research Service*. Washington, D. C.: U. S. Government Printing Office, 1976.

8. James P. Smith and F. Welch. "Inequality: Race Differences in the Distribution of Earnings." Mimeographed. University of California at Los Angeles, 1977.

9. Morton Paglin. "The Measurement and Trend of Inequality: A Basic Revision." *American Economic Review* 65: 598-609 (1975).

10. Benjamin Okner. "Total U. S. Tax Burdens: 1966 and 1970 Compared." Mimeographed. Washington, D. C.: U. S. Congressional Budget Office, 1976.

11. Morgan Reynolds and Eugene Smolensky. *Public Expenditures, Taxes and the Distribution of Income: The U. S., 1950, 1961, 1970*. Institute for Research on Poverty Monograph Series, 1977.

The Relationship of   3
Annual and Lifetime
Earnings

In the previous chapter we observed that family personal income tended to increase with age and that shifts in the age distribution might affect our measures or inequality of annual income. The distinction between annual and lifetime earnings may have even more important implications for our analysis of inequality and our understanding of how and why inequality exists.

Suppose we consider two individuals, both of whom have the following options open to them. In option 1 each one can receive $15,000 a year forever; in option 2 each one can receive $10,000 for one year and then, beginning one year from now, receive $15,500 forever. Further suppose that either one can borrow or lend any amount of money he wishes at an interest rate of 10% per year. Which option should be chosen by either or both of the two persons? As the problem is stated, each individual should be indifferent between the two options and could choose either 1 or 2. Why?

Suppose an individual chose option 2, with the irregular income pattern. He can convert this back to the even or constant income pattern by borrowing $5,000 at a 10% interest rate, or an interest charge of $500 per year. Then the individual who chose option 2 plus the loan would have available for consumption in each year income minus interest payments, or $15,000, the same amount as in option 1.

It is useful at this point to introduce the concept of the present discounted value (*PDV*) of the lifetime earnings stream.

PDV of Lifetime Earnings $=$ earnings$_{t=0}$

$$+ \frac{\text{earnings}_{t=1}}{(1+i)} + \frac{\text{earnings}_{t=2}}{(1+i)^2} \cdots$$

$$+ \frac{\text{earnings}_{t=N}}{(1+i)^N} = \sum_{j=0}^{N} \frac{N\,\text{earnings}_{t+j}}{(1+i)^j}$$

where i is the interest rate. With the earnings stream lasting forever, N equals infinity. In terms of the example, in option 1 the individual receives $15,000 a year. It is well known that

$$\sum_{j=0}^{\infty} x^t = \frac{1}{1-x}$$

if x is less than one (in absolute value). Let $x = 1/(1 + i)$. Therefore the PDV of option 1 is $15,000 $(\frac{1+i}{i})$ or $165,000. Now in option 2 the individual receives $10,000 the initial year and $15,000 in all the subsequent years. This can be written as

$$PDV_{\text{option 2}} = \$10,000 + (\frac{1}{1+i}) \sum_{j=0}^{\infty} \frac{\$15,500}{(1+i)^j}$$

$$= 10,000 + 155,000 = \$165,000$$

which is the same as the PDV of option 1.[1]

Suppose our economy consisted of only two individuals, A and B, who enter it at the same date. Then if both chose option 1, each would receive $15,000 a year. If they both chose option 2, each would receive $10,000 the first year and $15,000 in all subsequent years. In terms of annual income, there would be no inequality. However, if one chose option 1 and the other option 2, there would be inequality in annual income—$5,000 in the first year and $500 in each subsequent year. But while in this case there is inequality in annual income, both persons had the same options and both can enjoy exactly the same consumption as the other in each year. Thus, most economists would argue that even if one person chose option 1 and the other 2, there is no inequality. Put another way, the proper frame of reference for the measurement of inequality is the present discounted value of lifetime earnings, which may be distributed much differently than annual earnings.

---

1 In this example we find the PDV of the stream beginning in year 1 and then discount this PDV back to year zero.

1. Human Capital

The above contrived example contains the essential ingredients of the human capital theory, or at least that branch of human capital theory that argues that the economy is in equilibrium. To understand this model, let us assume that there is complete certainty about all future prices. Further, let us assume that in the marketplace a worker receives a real wage rate (W/P) equal to his marginal productivity. (To simplify matters, we can fix P at 1 and concentrate on W.) Marginal productivity is defined as the increase in output achieved by increasing labor or any other input by one unit. A person's marginal productivity may depend on the quantity of capital and other inputs with which he works. His marginal productivity may also depend on his level and combination of skills.

The combination of skills a person possesses is the result of the interplay of a variety of forces. One useful way of characterizing these factors is: initial or genetic endowments, parental or home environment, training provided by schools and the military, and training purchased by the individual outside the home and schools. Parental or home environment includes such diverse items as expenditures of money on diet and books; expenditures of time on teaching the ABCs; expenditures of love and affection on molding the child's personality; and expenditures of behavior which inculcate intended or unintended values. Similarly, schools can teach the child facts, develop his reasoning abilities and motor skills, and affect his behavioral skills.

Suppose we concentrate on schooling for the moment. If, by going to school longer, a person increases his skills and marginal productivity, then that person will gain an increase in his earnings. The increase in skills can be labeled an increase in human capital. In the next chapter we will consider the empirical evidence on the effectiveness of schooling in raising earnings. But at this point, we will explore in greater depth the insight the human capital model gives us in examining inequality in earnings.

Let us begin with a very simple model in which everyone has the same innate ability and parental environment. The differences in skills will arise only because of differences in schooling. Further, assume that schooling confers no other benefits on the individual. Now, let us examine the choices of an individual. If he stops schooling now, his skills are such that he can obtain $15,000 a year forever. If he goes to school for a year, he will become more skilled and will receive $15,500 a year forever. However, to go to school he must forgo either earnings or leisure. To simplify matters, assume that he forgoes earnings of $5,000 and that there are no additional costs of going to school.[2] Then, if the individual goes to school for one year, he will

---

2 In equilibrium the last unit of leisure taken equals his wage rate. Thus, any leisure forgone must be worth as much as lost income.

have an annual earnings stream of $10,000 for the first year and $15,500 in all subsequent years. We know from the contrived example at the beginning of this chapter that if the interest rate were 10% the individual should be indifferent between attending or not attending this one additional year of schooling. The student should also be able to show that if the market interest rate were less than 10%, the *PDV* of earnings with the extra year of schooling would exceed that of the *PDV* of earnings without schooling and that the individual would make a wise investment by going to school for one more year.

Now, suppose that the market rate of interest were 8%. Then this individual and many others like him would choose to obtain more education. As the supply of educated manpower increases, there is more "skilled" labor in the economy. The increase in the supply of "skilled" labor will cause the wage rates paid to "skilled" labor to decrease. Eventually, the *PDV* of earnings with and without the schooling calculated at the 8% interest rate will be equalized. Thus, an extremely important idea introduced by human capital theory is that wages adjust so that the present discounted value of earnings would be the same for people who can borrow at the same interest rate and who have equal ability prior to schooling.

Let the earnings a person would receive annually with zero (or the minimum) years of schooling be Y_0. It can be shown, with the assumptions set out above, that for any level of schooling above the minimum, annual earnings would be increased enough so that

$$\frac{Y_1 - Y_0}{Y_1} = iS_1 \tag{1}$$

where Y_1 is earnings when the person has S_1 years of schooling and i is the interest rate at which funds can be invested. The human capital model, as represented in this equation, states that annual wages adjust to make the rate of return on schooling equal to the market interest rate or to equalize the present discounted value of lifetime earnings.

Suppose we think of an economy in which different people have different abilities which are distributed normally, like the bell-shaped curve in Fig. 2.1. In the absence of schooling, the distribution of Y_0 would be proportional to the distribution of ability. However, the distribution of Y_1 differs from that of Y_0 because of the addition of the iS term. Thus, the human capital model can explain why earnings are not distributed normally.

More importantly, the model implies that since annual wage rates have adjusted to equalize the *PDV* of lifetime earnings over different schooling levels, the measures of inequality such as those in the previous chapter which are based on annual earnings are misleading. Other implications of this model can be obtained using a slightly different framework.

An individual can calculate the *PDV* of earnings for all levels of schooling and select the level of schooling which yields the highest *PDV*. An alternative way of stating this result is that the individual should calculate his rate of return on his investment (*r*) in schooling and continue to invest until *r* equals *i*, the market rate of interest.[3] As long as the extra skills produced by schooling become smaller (though remain positive) as schooling is increased, the rate of return on investment will decline.[4] This inverse relationship between *r* and years of schooling is given in Fig. 3.1 as the curve *DD*. This curve can be thought of as the demand curve for education. The supply curve, *SS*, in this figure would indicate how the cost of borrowing funds would vary with the schooling and the amount of funds borrowed. In Fig. 3.1, it is assumed that the individual can borrow all he wants at the same rate. In Fig. 3.1, the individual should invest *E** in years of schooling. In this diagram a person's annual earnings will be equal to the return on each year of schooling, or ODAE*, which is the total area under the demand curve.

Now let us ask why some people choose different amounts of schooling. Fig. 3.2 and 3.3 indicate the two possible sources for inequality in schooling. In Fig. 3.2, there are different demand curves for education by different people, but a common supply curve. In Fig. 3.3 there are different sup-

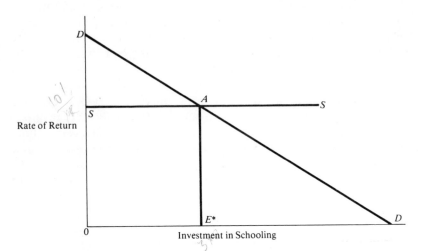

Fig. 3.1 Supply and Demand for Schooling.

---

3 There are a few instances in which this alternative rule does not yield the same, correct answer as the *PDV* rule.

4 That is, schooling is subject to diminishing marginal productivity.

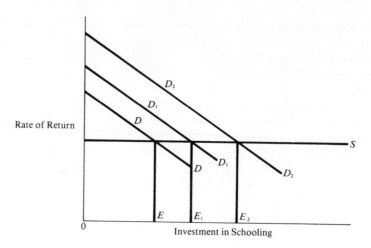

Fig. 3.2 Supply and Various Demand Curves for Schooling.

ply curves, but a common demand curve. In Fig. 3.2, all individuals receive the same rate of return on their investment in the last year of schooling, but choose different amounts of schooling and have different earnings
(the area under each person's demand curve). In Fig. 3.3, individuals can
borrow funds at different rates; thus, different levels of investment are optimal. In this figure, the shifting supply curve results in different levels of
schooling, annual earnings, and *PDV* of lifetime earnings. Obviously, it
would be possible to have another diagram with both supply and demand
curves varying by individual.

Why would supply or demand curves vary by individual? Consider,
first, the supply curves. Some people can be better credit risks than others
because they can convince lenders that loans to them entail less risk. For example, children from wealthier families may be able to pledge securities to a
bank, work in a family-owned business, or borrow funds cheaply from
their parents. All these reasons suggest that the supply curve for children
from wealthier and poorer families may be like SS and S_2S_2, respectively, in
Fig. 3.3.

Next consider the demand curves. It is certainly true that at any given
money wage rate for educated labor, some people derive non-wage-related
benefits from education and would demand more education than those who
do not derive such benefits. However, people should base their demand for
education on the total return. Thus, in Fig. 3.2, the demand curves will not
shift for this reason if the vertical axis refers to the total return.

Differential demand curves may arise because of differential abilities
obtained prior to starting school. We suggested earlier that schooling and

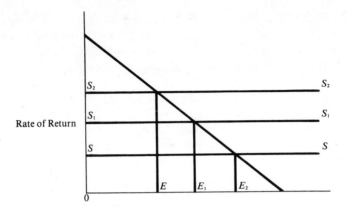

Fig. 3.3 Demand and Various Supply Curves for Schooling.

other abilities are combined to produce skill. Consider the following two different "production" functions:[5]

$$(1)\ \text{Skills} = \underline{d}\ \text{School} + b\ \text{Ability}$$
$$(2)\ \text{Skills} = \underline{c}\ \text{(School) (Ability)}$$

In the first, each extra year of schooling adds $\underline{d}$ units of skills. In the second, each extra unit of school adds c (Ability) units of skills. With the second production function, the addition to skills will be greater the higher the level of ability. Thus, more able people would find that schooling added more to their skills and to their income, and they would, therefore, demand more schooling. Such differences in ability arise because of differences in genetic endowments or in family environment. Becker [1] labels the variation in demand curves arising from production function 2 as the "differential capacity" model.

It seems appropriate to call differences in income arising from variation in supply curves "inequality in opportunity." Note that this concept includes low family income leading to lesser abilities because of poor nutrition, since families are constrained from borrowing to pay for the nutrition.

2. The On-the-job Training Model

The human capital model also contains another important reason why inequality in annual earnings may be a very poor guide to inequality in *PDV* of lifetime earnings. Many firms provide on-the-job training to their em-

---

5 There is little evidence available to suggest which of the two production functions is correct.

ployees. Such training may be specific or general. Specific training is usable only in that firm. General training is usable in other firms. For simplicity, let us concentrate on the general training model. Such training increases a person's marginal productivity, which will raise his wage rate in a competitive market.

Suppose, therefore, an individual entering the job market is offered the same position with two firms. Suppose also that the individual is offered the same starting wage in both firms and that all the nonwage aspects of the two firms are identical. Further, suppose the individual knows with certainty that firm 1 will not provide him with any training while firm 2 will provide him with general training over a period of years. Thus, the options open to the individual are described by the age earnings profile labeled 1 and 2 in Fig. 3.4. Under the conditions set forth, the individual would choose firm 2 and receive a higher *PDV* of lifetime earnings.

But the story does not end here. Suppose the individual we have been discussing is like many others, all of whom can enter firm 1 or 2. Each of them will come to firm 2 who will learn that it can lower starting and subsequent wages and still attract workers. Indeed, firm 2 can lower starting wages until the present discounted value of the lifetime earnings stream it offers just equals the *PDV* of the earnings stream given by firm 1.[6] The earnings profile labeled 3 shows the results of such an adjustment. Both 3 and 1 have the same *PDV*, but there will be inequality in annual earnings.

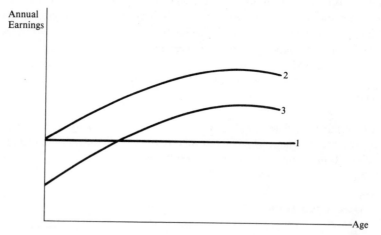

Fig. 3.4 Hypothetical Age Earnings Profiles.

---

6 If training the worker requires resources, firm 2 will have to offer the lower starting wages to recapture the investment cost, all of whose returns accrue to the worker.

3. Critique of the Human Capital/On-the-job Training Model

The human capital model provides some rather strong results. These were, of course, obtained by making some rather strong assumptions. If the strong assumptions are altered many of the specific conclusions in the model will be changed, but the flavor will remain. For example, if some of the individual's benefits of education occur outside the labor market, equation (1) in this chapter need not be valid. But it would still be true that if education increases labor market skills, earnings will be related to education.

It is also true that uncertainty over future wage rates can affect decisions about investment in education and on-the-job training. Moreover, unexpected developments may mean that observed differences in earnings by education level some 30 years after the completion of schooling do not resemble the anticipated differences.

There is, in addition, a more subtle criticism of this model. In our discussion of the human capital model, we noted that if the supply-of-funds and demand-for-education curves differ by individual, different persons would receive different rates of return for the same investment in schooling. (A similar result would hold in the on-the-job training model.) The student will recall, however, that equilibrium was obtained by the market adjusting wage rates by occupation or skill level. If the market cannot do more than distinguish people by their eduction level, the market cannot adjust wages so that the rate of return from investment is equal to the cost of borrowing financial capital for each person. In other words, full equilibrium and the results based upon it, including the relationship between annual and lifetime earnings, cannot hold fully. The human capital model, nevertheless, provides a useful way to think about problems associated with the distribution of annual and lifetime earnings.

REFERENCES

1. Gary Becker. "Human Capital and the Personal Distribution of Income: An Analytical Approach," in *Human Capital Second Edition*. New York: National Bureau of Economic Research, 1975.

Education 4
and
Earnings

Even during the nineteenth and early twentieth centuries, education was thought of as a means of increasing skills and earnings.[1] However, it was during the 1960s that formal schooling (elementary, high school, and college) and vocational education were trumpeted as effective and crucial tools in eliminating poverty and equalizing the distribution of earnings. In 1964, Samuelson [2], for example, stated: "How do education and training affect lifetime income? Are they worth their cost? The evidence answers, 'Decidedly yes'" (p. 118). Samuelson's evidence was based primarily on the relationship between education and earnings. Since his writing the enthusiasm for education leading to large increases in earnings has cooled though there is growing evidence that education has nonwage effects that might make the rate of return to education competitive with returns on other investments.

In this chapter we will assess the evidence on the relationship of education to earnings. In most of the chapter, we will equate education with formal schooling but will consider some of the evidence on vocational schooling. We will first consider the information available from the U.S. Bureau of the Census, which collects data on education, earnings, and other variables from a random sample of the population. While this data source provides much valuable information, it has several potentially major difficulties. First, there is an empirical question of whether the difference in earnings between the more and the less educated should be attributed solely to education or whether part is attributable to differences in "ability" of the more educated. Second, there is a question of whether observed differences in earnings of the more educated (adjusted for ability) will apply if there is a major increase in the supply of educated labor. Both these issues will be explored in some detail later in the chapter.

---

1. For example, see Gorseline [1].

1. Age Earnings Profiles by Education Level

The U.S. Census Bureau has been collecting data on age, education, and earnings since 1940. While many of the particular results on schooling and earnings vary from census to census, there is enough similarity that we can concentrate on the results in only one census sample. The 1960 census has been extensively examined by Mincer [3] and others. Mincer has calculated and charted the average earnings of individuals at various ages with particular years of completed schooling. Figure 4.1 reproduces his chart for

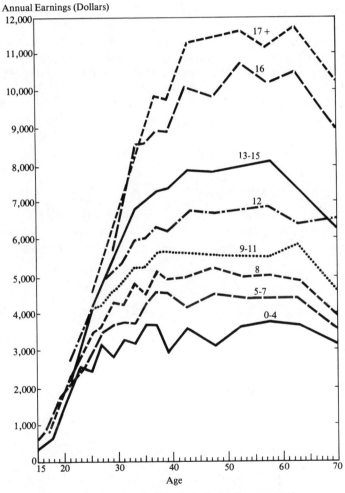

NOTE: Figures on curves indicate years of schooling completed.

Fig. 4.1 Annual Earnings Classified by Years of Age, for Indicated Schooling Groups. (**Source:** 1/1,000 sample of U. S. Census, 1960, Mincer [3], p. 66.)

white, nonfarm men. Several things stand out in Fig. 4.1. First, starting salaries for many of the education groups are about the same. Second, the age earnings profiles increase steeply for the first decade after each education group begins to work but is fairly level after age 40 till about age 60. Third, the profiles are steeper for the more educated. Finally, in the 40 to 50 age bracket there are large differences in earnings between education levels.

The earnings profile for any education level in Fig. 4.1 is based on men surveyed in 1960 and clearly refers to individuals at each age level. But under certain assumptions, which need not be valid, we can use the information in Fig. 4.1 to calculate what a given group of men with a given education level will earn throughout their career. For example, we can assume that high school graduates aged 30 are on average alike in all respects (except age) to high school graduates aged 20. We can also assume that on average, earnings by education level will increase at the same proportion as average wages grow in the economy. With these and other assumptions, we can calculate the difference in earnings annually for, say, a high school and a college graduate. This difference is shown in Fig. 4.2.

If we assume that the only benefits of schooling are extra wages, and if we know the cost of schooling, we can calculate the rate of return to schooling. That is, the rate of return is the interest rate, r, such that

$$\sum_{t=0}^{N} \frac{\triangle Y_t - C_t}{(1 + r)^t} = 0$$

Here $\triangle Y$ is the difference in earnings, C_t is the cost of education, and N is year of retirement or death. The costs of education include tuition net of scholarship, books, and extra living expenses. Earnings forgone from not

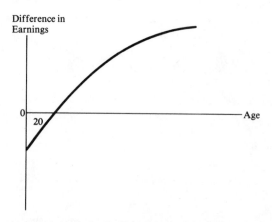

Fig. 4.2 Average College Graduate Earnings Minus Average High School Graduate Earnings.

working are often treated as a cost but in Fig. 4.2 are given the equivalent treatment of a negative benefit.

Many economists have used a method similar to that sketched above to calculate the rate of return on investment in schooling. Using the 1960 census, Mincer [3] calculates the before-tax rate of return to an individual from high school graduation at about 13% and from college graduation at about 10%.

Estimates based on the 1940 and the 1950 census give generally comparable results. For example, in Table 4.1, which is reproduced from Hansen's study of 1949 earnings gathered in the 1950 census, the before-tax rate of return from ninth to twelfth grade for males is 15.3%. In the 1970s the job prospects of the more educated have not been as rosy. From 1969 to 1974 according to Freeman [5], starting salaries of college graduates went up less rapidly than the price level and less rapidly than annual earnings of full-time workers. While the recent poor performance of college graduates may be a temporary phenomenon, Freeman has calculated that the rate of return to *college education* may have declined by 30%, for example, from 11 1/2 in 1969 to 8 1/2 in 1974.

2. The Ability Problem

As noted earlier, the results in the previous section have been questioned on empirical and theoretical grounds. A basic empirical complaint is that the use of average earnings by education level (for given age) is appropriate only if on average the more and the less educated are alike in all other respects that determine earnings. Put another way, it is often argued that the more educated are also more "able" irrespective of education and that part of the observed differences in earnings by education level is attributable to ability.

A wide variety of skills or abilities can be used to earn a living. This multitude of skills can include cognitive abilities such as memory, logical reasoning, knowledge of chemistry, and verbal fluency. Other labor market skills may be noncognitive, such as a strong back, leadership, dexterity, and coordination.

Not surprisingly, college professors of economics are aware that brighter people are more likely to go to college. Thus, much effort has been spent to try to adjust earnings data in the census and other studies for the differences in cognitive skills as measured by IQ or other tests. Before examinating this issue, it is worth emphasizing that the other types of ability may also differ by education level, and controlling for them may be important as will be seen later.

In order for IQ or any other type of ability to account for part of the observed differences in earnings by education level, two conditions must be met. The ability must be related to earnings and must vary by education

Table 4.1 Internal rates of return to private resource investment in schooling, before tax, United States, males 1949.*

From:			(1)	(2)	(3)	(4)	(5)	(6)	(7)
To:	Age		6	8	12	14	16	18	20
		Grade	1	3	7	9	11	13	15
(1)	7	2	†						
(2)	11	6	†	†					
(3)	13	8	†	†	†				
(4)	15	10	28.3	34.6	25.9	12.7			
(5)	17	12	25.6	29.4	25.3	15.3	18.6		
(6)	19	14	18.1	18.7	14.8	10.4	9.5	6.2	
(7)	21	16	18.2	18.7	16.2	12.9	13.0	11.6	18.7

Source: Hansen [4].

*All rate-of-return figures are subject to some error, since the estimation to one decimal place had to be made by interpolation between whole percentage figures.

†This indicates an infinite rate-of-return, given the assumption that education is costless to the individual to the completion of eighth grade.

level. Ample evidence exists that those with more education are brighter, irrespective of education. There are also a number of studies that measure the effect of IQ on earnings. Unfortunately, none of these studies is a random sample but is restricted to some particular portion of the U.S. population. Moreover, the various studies use a multitude of tests to approximate IQ. Some of these tests may be more reliable than others, and some may represent different cognitive or noncognitive skills.[2]

Suppose, however, we lump all the results together. Then it seems to the author that there is a noticeable and interesting pattern to the results. For simplicity assume there are only two levels of ability. Then the various studies suggest that there is an age earnings profile by ability level like that shown in Fig. 4.3. That is, at the beginning of the working life, high- and low-ability people (alike in other respects) earn the same amount, but earnings grow much faster for the more able.[3] Since there is no difference in

---

2 For example, several studies use armed forces qualification tests which contain material on mechanical aptitude.

3 For studies when people are early in their career, see Griliches and Mason, [6], Wolfle and Smith [7], and Sewell and Hauser [8]. Studies later in the career include Olneck [9], and Blum and Coleman [10]. A few studies including Taubman and Wales [11], Sewell and Hauser [8], and Fägerlind [12] contain earnings at several ages. These latter studies are consistent with the pattern in Fig. 4.3.

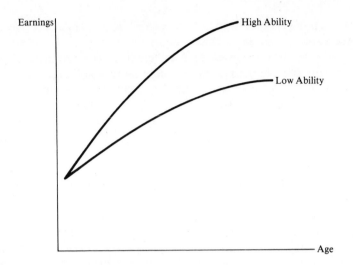

Fig. 4.3 Synthetic Age Earnings Profiles by Ability Level.

earnings by IQ when people begin to work, none of the small difference in earnings by educational level is attributale to cognitive ability. Later in the career, however, part of the observed earnings differential by education level is properly attributable to cognitive skills; some estimates in Fägerlind Olneck [9], and Taubman and Wales [11] suggest a bias of about 25% to 30% when the person has about 15 years of work experience.

The student may wonder why the effect of IQ increases with experience. One possible answer is that more able people are willing to invest voluntarily in on-the-job training. As indicated in the previous chapter, such investment may be paid for by temporarily lowering observed wages. However, an alternative possibility related to uncertainty is more appealing to the author. Suppose firms have difficulty determining in advance who the good or talented workers are. Then firms may promote workers on the basis of past performance. Higher IQ workers are on average more able, are promoted more quickly to more important positions, and are given more training by firms; as a result, their earnings increase faster than do the earnings of their less able co-workers.

While most attention in economics has focused on cognitive abilities, it has always been recognized that noncognitive skills, including leadership and strength, may also account for part of the observed effect of education on earnings. Unfortunately, most samples have little or no direct information on such noncognitive skills. Suppose, however, such noncognitive skills are either produced by, say, parental income or are related to parental education or other observed family background variables. Then it is possible to adjust partially the observed education effects by eliminating (or controlling for) the effects of differences in parental income, education, etc.

At this point is is useful to introduce a distinction which will play a more important role in the next chapter. A variable such as intelligence or ability may affect earnings directly (because the person is more productive) and indirectly (by causing the person to obtain more schooling). The previous results for IQ have referred to the direct effects on earnings primarily because only if the direct effects of a variable are nonzero can we misattribute to education the effect of ability. Thus, we will continue for the time being the practice of examining only the direct effects of parental income and ignoring the indirect effects.

There is a great hodgepodge of results available on the effects of controlling for family background. A huge variety of different aspects of family background have been used in the various studies. A highly impressionistic summary of these studies would suggest that, as with IQ and education, most variables have little or no effect early in a person's career but that some variables have quite strong direct effects after 8 to 10 years of work experience. Among the variables that have direct effects are parental income when the offspring was about 14, religious background, and family size.[4] Even ignoring indirect effects via education and measured cognitive ability, those people from richer families, from Catholic or Jewish families, and from smaller families earn more, and these effects apparently persist at least till age 50.

We can think of a wide variety of skills being related to the above background variables; for example, confidence, leadership, motivation, and drive. But it seems likely that the background variables used would be very imprecise indicators of leadership, and the like. Recently a different approach to the problem has been taken. Suppose we think of an individual's skills being produced by combining genetic endowments with family and other environments. If we can adjust or control for these productive agents, we can estimate the true impact of education on earnings. Data on identical twins allow us to eliminate differences in genetic endowments and much of family environment. The one study available, which is for white male twins about 50 years old, indicates that as much as 2/3 of the observed differences in earnings-by-education level is attributable to differences in "ability."[5] There are technical reasons for suspecting that the estimate that 2/3 of the observed effect of education is due to ability is overstated and that a figure of about 45% is more reasonable. Recently Behrman et al. [15] have examined earnings equations for a subset of the same sample for whom an IQ-type test is available. They find that if the twins are treated as individuals, holding constant IQ reduces the education coefficient by about

---

4 See for example, Sewell and Hauser [8], and Taubman [12].

5 See Taubman [14].

30% and that adding measures of family background to the equation reduces the same coefficient another 5%. Taking the 45% bias on education from holding all genetic and family environments constant as a reference point, their results suggest that cognitive skills account for about 2/3 of the ability bias, with the rest arising from noncognitive skills. (As explained in Chapter 5, this does not indicate the relative contributions of cognitive and noncognitive skills to the inequality of earnings.) This same study also suggests that the rate of return to education (based on earnings alone) is no more than 3% to 4%. This is, of course, low compared with returns available to individuals even in savings accounts. However, even if this finding is verified in other samples, we cannot conclude that schooling is a "bad" investment, since only the wage benefits have been included in the calculations.

While currently there are no other studies of identical twins available which contain data on earnings, there are several samples of brothers. These brother studies also suggest that parental education and the other readily available measures for family background and ability are highly imperfect proxies to estimate the contribution of family background to earnings and to control for differences in family background when estimating the effect of schooling on earnings.[6]

Based on these twin studies and brother studies, it seems likely that a substantial portion of the differences in earnings-by-education level is not properly attributable to education.

3. Women and Blacks

The above results on the effects of education on earnings are based primarily on samples of white males who constitute a minority of the U.S. population and about one half of the working force. Because of discrimination in the labor market or because of differential abilities and/or environments, blacks and white women need not receive the same wage benefits from education.

The census, of course, contains information on earnings by education level for women. This data source, however, is even less useful for studying the wage returns to education than for males. While under current institutional arrangements, most men between 25 and 55 are in the labor force, many women choose to do housework. Presumably a woman who chooses to do work in the marketplace finds her marginal productivity and pecuni-

---

6 See Olneck [9]. However, for a contrary view see Chamberlain and Griliches [16]. That the usual proxies for family background are inadequate is the conclusion reached in studies of educational attainment and/or IQ in Jencks and Brown [17] and in Sewell and Hauser [18].

ary and nonpecuniary rewards from working there greater than from working in the house. Those who choose not to work in the marketplace may be those with below-average marginal productivity in the market. The labor-force participation rate for women varies by education level. Thus, using data solely on the women observed at work may yield biased estimates of the effect of education for all women. Another difficulty with using census data to examine the returns from education is that women currently at work may not have worked continuously but may have spent some years having and raising a family. The human capital model in the previous chapter suggests that dropping out of the labor market reduces investment in on-the-job training. The loss in experience need not be the same at all education levels, but the census does not have the necessary data to calculate such loss in experience.

Using a different sample, Mincer and Polachek [19] are able to calculate the years of work experience in the marketplace lost in having and rearing children. As suggested, the figures differ by education level. They indicate that using the more accurate experience variable lets them explain the earnings data better. Their estimate of the effects of education on earnings for white women, with experience held constant, is about the same as those generally obtained for white men when hours and weeks worked are not included. But it is somewhat less than the usual results for males when these two variables are included which converts the equation into one for wage rates. If hours and weeks worked represent voluntary labor-leisure choices, then the wage rate is the proper one to study. Mincer and Polachek do not, however, adjust their estimates for the selectivity problem on women who are never in the labor market.

The census also has information on education and earnings for blacks. Analysis and interpretetation of these data are subject not only to the usual ability problems but also to problems relating to discrimination.

Discrimination in the labor market is generally defined as a group of individuals with certain identifying characteristics receiving a lifetime wage less than their lifetime marginal product. Such discrimination could be measured by comparing the earnings of equally skilled blacks and whites. Unfortunately, it is difficult to demonstrate that blacks and whites are equally skilled, since for example many blacks and whites went to different schools, and both Welch [20] and Freeman [21] indicate that blacks received lower quality schooling.

It is possible for the degree of discimination to vary over time and by schooling level. Both Freeman [21] and Welch and Smith [22] indicate that more educated blacks who graduated in 1970 or later receive more earnings relative to whites than, say, in 1960. At least for younger men it now appears that the effect of education on earnings is about the same for blacks and whites.

4. Vocational Training

The formal school system is not the only institution that provides training in skills used in the labor market. Individuals can also receive vocational training either from their employer or from a variety of vocational schools and institutions that do not offer formal degrees, for example, from secretarial and electronic schools. While there is very little analysis of particular training courses provided by employers, there are a number of studies of vocational training programs provided or financed by the governement either through the Manpower Development Training Act (MDTA) or the GI Bill. These studies have calculated earnings after completion of the vocational training.

While it is relatively easy to calculate the posttraining earnings, it is not as easy to calculate what the trainee would have earned in the absence of training. While in one sense this difficulty can be thought of as "how able" the trainees are, there is an additional complication. There are incentives for those who are already doing poorly—given schooling, IQ, and so on—in the job market to enter the program since they will forgo less earnings. Moreover, most of the vocational programs studied are ones in which the government pays a stipend to participants. The stipend is more attractive the less one can earn in the market.

O'Neill and Ross [23] in a study of the GI Bill, which uses some sophisticated though apparently incomplete efforts to overcome these difficulties, estimate an increase in annual earnings of about 10% per year in 1972–74 for those veterans who entered vocational training in 1969 and terminated training in 1971. Of course depending on the costs of the program a 10% increase in annual earnings that lasts throughout a person's career can be greater or less than a 10% rate of return. The data in O'Neill and Ross on forgone earnings and other data on tuition costs of such training suggest a rate of return around 10%, but of course this estimate is sensitive to the calculation of what earnings would be without training.

5. Screening and Signaling Models

Much of the economic research on education and earnings in the past 15 years has been based on a (human capital) model in which education increases wages because it increases skills. More recently some economists have begun to question the "because" clause. The alternative model proposed by these economists, is, it its most extreme form, one in which education does not increase skills one bit but merely identifies those individuals with higher preexisting skills.

This "signaling" model, as well as a somewhat different variant which can be labeled "screening," have some important though not necessarily obvious implications. To see these implications, let us examine a pure signaling model as developed by Spence [24]. Suppose that firms produce output by combining capital with two grades of labor, denoted A and B. Suppose further that firms find it difficult to test beforehand whether a worker is type A or type B and that firms are precluded from either measuring on-the-job performance or reassigning a worker once he is hired. Also assume that the firm knows that the annual marginal product of type A workers is 1 and that of type B workers is 2, which output can be sold at a price of $1.00 each. Finally assume it is known that in the population, 3/4 of the workers are A's and 1/4 are B's. If the firm cannot distinguish A from B workers, it should be willing to pay each worker his *expected* marginal product, which would be $3/4 (1) + 1/4 (2) = \$1 \ 1/4 \ (\$1.25)$. Next, suppose that the firm offers to pay educated people $1.50 and noneducated people $1.00. To simplify matters assume education is tuition free and that to become an educated worker an A person must spend two years in school while a B person can master the curriculum in one year. Consider the options open to the type A and B workers. If an A worker opts to become educated, he must forgo $2.00 worth of earnings while a B worker must forego $1.00. Since once educated the extra income would be the same for A and B workers, educated B workers with the lower costs would receive a higher rate of return than an educated A worker.

It certainly would be possible for the rate of return to be greater than the interest rate for B workers but less than the interest rate for A workers. Indeed, firms can manipulate the wage offered to skilled workers, setting it between the marginal product of A and B workers till only B workers would find it worthwhile to obtain the education.

The pure signaling model suggests that people will voluntarily sort themselves into groups with different skills or, in other words, identify their skill levels. To be a valid representation of the world, the model requires among other things that firms not be able to identify skills in a less costly way by prejob tests nor be able to determine actual work done on a job.

A screening model can be thought of as a variation of the signaling model. The basic idea of a screening model is that ability useful to the employer in a given occupation is thought to vary with schooling. Employers know that a greater percentage of the more educated have the skills they are looking for in better paying and more productive occupations. Suppose putting the wrong person on the job is costly because resources must be used to hire and fire him and because the wrong person can ruin the output of others. Thus, classifying people on the basis of imperfect prejob tests may be costly. To save on these costs, firms will try to interview and try out people whom the firm thinks will have the appropriate skills.

Till now this model seems very like the signaling model. Suppose, however, firms know that as labor markets tighten (unemployment falls) they are likely to interview the less able portion of the more educated. Then it becomes more profitable for firms to interview and hire some of the less educated for a given job. Once firms identify the more able members of the less educated group, there would be no reason to fire them when unemployment became greater. Cyclical variation thus allows some of the less educated to pass the education screen. Then a comparison of the more and the less educated within the occupations that use education as a screen would allow us to calculate the impact of education on marginal productivity—provided non-schooling-based ability is the same for the two education groups.

Within-occupation equations can be used to calculate the distribution of earnings in various occupations for various education levels. Let us assume that people will choose the occupation which maximizes their income. The information on earnings calculated within occupation can be used to see if more people with less education would freely choose occupations of the managerial kind. Using this technique, Taubman and Wales [11] have calculated that many high school graduates (of 1938 to 1945) may have been screened out of preferred occupations and that up to one half of the (adjusted) effects of education on earnings were due to screening. Their calculations, however, are sensitive to at least two assumptions. The first is that within occupations the more and the less educated are equally able (except for IQ or any other ability created by schooling). The second is that the less educated who could have made more in the managerial occupation were excluded from this occupation rather than voluntarily choosing another occupation with lower wages but supplemented by nonmonetary rewards desirable to them.

It is difficult to determine what proportion of wage effects of education is attributable to productivity increase and to signaling or screening. But suppose that signaling or screening is an important element. What difference does it make? A person's calculation of his rate ot return to education and his position in the income distribution would be unchanged whether education increased productivity or acted as a screen. Thus, in estimating what has been the rate of return to education *to an individual* or what have been the effects of schooling on the distribution of earnings, it is not necessary to distinguish between productivity and signaling effects.

Such a distinction is necessary, however, when calculating either the return to society from education or the impact of a major new educational program. To society the rate of return should be based on the increase in total output and the total costs arising from more education. In the pure signaling model, there was no increase in output but only a redistribution of income when *B* workers became more educated. When there are many occupations and firms have to sort people into the right position, better information may allow firms to sort better and increase output. If education both increases productivity and acts as a screen, the social return to education should be based on the output without the added education but with the next best screening device used and on the equity of the income distribution. The cost to society, then, would be the full resources used in the educational process minus the resource cost of running the next best screening device. It is not obvious that the social return to schooling is more or less than the private return.

There is another important difference between the productivity and signaling models. Let there be a major governmental program to increase the education level so that each person has a college degree. If education were purely a signaling device, this program would not increase output and would have a negative social and private rate of return.

6. Adjustments to Shifts in Supply and Demand

Most of the studies on the effects of education on income are based on differences in earnings in a cross section of individuals. Even ignoring the possibility that some of the observed differences in earnings may be caused by differences in unobserved ability correlated with education, these cross-section findings will not indicate what would be the returns to education if there were a policy that shifted the supply or the demand curve for a large group of people.

Fig. 4.4, which is based on the material in Chapter 3, section 1, contains the supply and demand curves for education for a representative individual. The same curves are assumed to apply to many people. Suppose that a government loan policy were to shift the supply curve for this (and the other) individuals from SS to S_1S_1. Such a shift would alter the equilibrium level of education and the equilibrium rate of return. Yet from Chapter 3 we know

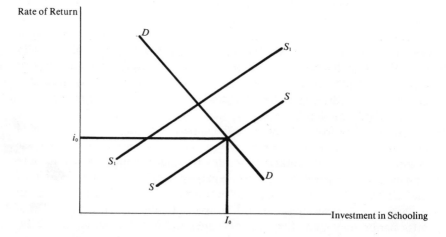

Fig. 4.4 Hypothetical Supply and Demand Curves for Educational Investment.

that in equilibrium $(Y_1 - Y_0)/Y_1$ equals $i(S_1 - S_0)$. Since the equilibrium level of i has changed, the percentage difference between Y_1 and Y_0 will alter. As argued in Chapter 3, Y_1 and Y_0 will respond to shifts in the supplies of variously educated groups of people till equilibrium is restored. Thus, more educated people will receive a lower return from education after the loan policy than before. In the simple case where there are no differences in ability and no other adjustments in the economic system, wages will adjust till the above equilibrium condition holds for all individuals. However, as noted at the end of Chapter 3, the extent of the adjustment is much more complex and uncertain when there are individual differences in ability and in financial capability.

At the beginning of this chapter, we indicated that from 1940 to about 1970 rates of return were approximately constant (but may have dropped since then).[7] During this period, educational attainment increased sharply. For example, the average education level of white males went from about 10 to 13 years. Why, then, did the return remain constant, and why does it seem to have dropped so suddenly after 1970?

Several answers have been advanced to these questions. One answer, of course, is that the economic models used to study earnings are incorrect. An answer economists find more acceptable is that those statements about increases in the supply of education leading to a reduced wage for the more educated assume that the demand for educated manpower has remained constant. From 1940 to 1970 demand may have increased enough to offset the effects of increased supply. Demand may have increased because of new technologies that utilize more educated people, because of the increase in the size and complexity of the stock of physical capital, and/or because of a shift in type of goods demanded as the economy evolved. One intriguing point raised by Freeman [5] is that from the early 1950s to the late 1960s the rapid expansion in the college system required more and more teachers. He has calculated that the supply of college graduates net of those teaching in college did not expand rapidly till about 1970. Then, partly because of the leveling off of the numbers of 18-to-24-year-olds, enrollment at colleges leveled off and colleges cut back sharply on the teachers they were hiring, whence the supply of college graduates available to the rest of the market expanded rapidly.

7. Summary

In this chapter we have found that the more educated receive more earnings than the less educated. When no adjustments are made for ability and no

---

7 A recent unpublished study indicates that the return may have fallen for high school graduates but that this fall was masked by differences in the construction of the census samples in 1940 and in subsequent years.

account is taken of nonwage returns and costs, the rate of return to college education is about 10%, with a higher rate for lower education levels. The amount needed to adjust for ability is subject to debate. When ability is equated to IQ, the adjustment is no more than 10% in the early years of work experience but as much as 30% later on. When more comprehensive measures of ability are used, an adjustment of 45% to 65% has been suggested.

The available evidence does not enable us to distinguish sharply between the idea that education increases productivity versus the idea that education acts as a signal of greater preexisting ability. For many purposes, however, this distinction is not needed.

REFERENCES

1. Donald E. Gorseline. *The Effect of Schooling Upon Income.* Bloomington: University of Indiana Press, 1932.

2. Paul Samuelson. *Principles of Economics.* New York: McGraw-Hill, 1964.

3. Jacob Mincer. *Schooling, Experience and Earnings.* New York: National Bureau of Economic Research, 1974.

4. W. Lee Hansen. "Total and Private Rates of Return to Investment in Schooling." *Journal of Political Economy* 71: 128 – 40 (1963).

5. Richard Freeman. "Overinvestment in College Training?" *Journal of Human Resources* 10:212 – 31 (1975).

6. Zvi Griliches and William Mason. "Education, Income and Ability." *Journal of Political Economy.* 80: S74 – 103 (1972).

7. Dael Wolfle and Joseph Smith. "The Occupational Value of Education for Superior High School Graduates." *Journal of Higher Education* 27:201 – 13 (1956).

8. William Sewell and Robert Hauser. *Education, Occupation, and Earnings: Achievement in the Early Career.* New York: Academic Press, 1975

9. Michael Olneck. "On the Use of Sibling Data to Estimate the Effects of Family Background, Cognitive Skills and Schooling: Results from the Kalamazoo Brothers Study." In *Kinometrics: Determinants of Socioeconomic Success Within and Between Families,* edited by Paul Taubman. Amsterdam: North Holland, 1977.

10. Zahava Blum and James Coleman. *Longitudinal Effects of Education on the Incomes and Occupational Prestige of Blacks and Whites.* Report Number 70, Baltimore: Center for the Study of Social Organization of Schools, Johns Hopkins University, 1970.

11. Paul Taubman and Terence Wales. "Higher Education, Mental Ability and Screening." *Journal of Political Economy* 81: 28 – 55 (1973).

12. Ingemar Fägerlund. *Formal Education and Adult Earnings.* Stockholm: Almqvist and Wicksell, 1975.

13. Paul Taubman. *Sources of Inequality of Earnings.* Amsterdam: North Holland, 1975.

14. Paul Taubman. "Earnings, Education, Genetics and Environment." *Journal of Human Resources* 11: 447 – 61 (1976).

15. Jere Behrman et al. "Inter and Intragenerational Determinants of Socioeconomic Success: Genetics, Family and Other Environments." mimeographed. University of Pennsylvania, 1977.

16. Gary Chamberlain and Zvi Griliches. "More on Brothers." In *Kinometrics: Determinants of Socioeconomic Success Within and Between Families,* edited by Paul Taubman. Amsterdam: North Holland, 1977.

17. Christopher Jencks and Marsha Brown. "Genes and Social Stratification: A Methodological Exploration with Illustrative Data." In *Kinometrics: Determinants of Socioeconomic Success Within and Between Families,* edited Paul Taubman. Amsterdam: North Holland, 1977.

18. William Sewell and Robert Hauser. "On the Effects of Family and Family Structure on Achievement." In *Kinometrics: Determinants of Socioeconomic Success Within and Between Families,* edited by Paul Taubman. Amsterdam: North Holland, 1977.

19. Jacob Mincer and Solomon Polachek. "Family Investments in Human Capital: Earnings of Women." *Journal of Political Economy* 82: S76 – 108 (1974).

20. Finis Welch. "Black-White Returns of Schooling." *American Economic Review* 63: 893 – 907 (1973).

21. Richard Freeman. "The Changing Labor Market for Minorities." In *Higher Education and the Labor Market,* edited by Margaret Gordon. New York: McGraw-Hill, 1974.

22. Finis Welch and James Smith. *Black-White Male Earnings and Employment: 1960-1970,* R-1666-DOL, Santa Monica: The Rand Corporation, July 1975.

23. David O'Neill and Sue Goetz Ross. *Voucher Funding of Training: A Study of the GI Bill,* PRI 312-76. Arlington: Public Research Institute, 1976.

24. A. Michael Spence. *Market Signaling: Informational Transfers in Hiring and Related Screening Processes.* Cambridge, Mass.: Harvard University Press, 1974.

The Role of Parents 5
in the Distribution of Income

In this chapter we will be concerned with describing and to a limited extent estimating the effects of parents on the distribution of income and earnings. We will be interested in how and why parents affect the average level and distribution of earnings of their children. In Chapter 6 we will be concerned with the general issue of "social mobility," which is roughly defined as the degree to which parents' income is *not* passed on to their children. As we shall see, social mobility is not exactly the mirror image of the effects of parents on their children's income potential.

A basic organizing framework of the previous chapters was that a person's skill level was "produced" by combining genetic endowments with various elements in the environment. In Chapter 4 we tried to estimate the effects of one aspect of the environment—schooling. In this chapter we shall be concerned with the effects of such items as genetic endowments and of family and other environments. We will try to quantify the importance of each of these aggregate categories. We will also try to examine how and why some parts of environment affect earnings capacity.

Before embarking on this task, a brief digression is necessary. In recent years, Jensen [1] and others have been concerned with estimating the effect of genetics on the distribution of intelligence and the average genetic level of intelligence for various races. The discussion of this emotional topic has been heated, to say the least. The heat, moreover, has tended to obscure some important points.

Suppose we have a group of people born and brought up at a particular time in a particular set of environments. There are available certain statistical techniques, whose appropriateness depends upon certain assumptions being true, which can be used to estimate what proportion of observed *variance* in IQ, earnings, or any other variable is attributable to genetic endowments or to family and other environments.[1] Now, suppose we are lucky enough to have the data and the right circumstances to make these estimates. What do we know? We know history, that is, we know the relative size of the variation in genetics and environment given the then existing distributions of genetics and environments. If in this historical period everyone had exactly the same environment, then genetics would have accounted for all the variation in IQ or earnings. Even if the distribution of genetic endowments and the prices attached to these remain fixed in the future, the distribution of earnings and the relative contribution of genetics can change if the distribution of environment alters, as will be shown below.

Much of the anger in the IQ debate has occurred because of Jensen's and others' conclusions that on average blacks have "poorer genes." This last phrase can best be understood by examining the following equation, in which IQ is produced by genetic endowments (G) and environment (N), and in which G and N are scaled so that they have coefficients of 1.

$$IQ = G + N \tag{1}$$

It is possible to calculate the average IQ on a given test for members of any group—though defining precisely who belongs in a group such as black or white may be difficult. Let an average be represented by a bar, for example, $\overline{IQ}$. The average IQ for this group will be given by

$$\overline{IQ} = \overline{G} + \overline{N} \tag{2}$$

By poorer genes, it is meant that $\overline{G}$ for blacks is smaller than $\overline{G}$ for whites.

The available data indicate that $\overline{IQ}$ is smaller for blacks than for whites. This difference in average IQ can occur because of cultural bias (i. e., items on the test depend on material with which whites are more familiar), or because of differences in either $\overline{G}$ or $\overline{N}$.

Most of the early "evidence" from which Jensen reached his conclusion that $\overline{G}$ was less for blacks was derived from estimates of the relative contribution of the variance of G and of N to IQ.[2]

However, information on the contribution of G and N to the variance of Y is not at all informative on $\overline{G}$ and $\overline{N}$. It is quite possible for the variance in N to be relatively small within groups but for $\overline{N}$ to vary greatly between

---

1 The variance is a measure of dispersion (or inequality) in a distribution. The variance is defined as the average squared difference between each observation and the average of the distribution. Variance $X = \frac{1}{N-1} \Sigma (X_i - \overline{X})^2$ where X_i are the individual values, $\overline{X}$ is the average, and N is the sample size.

2 The variance is a measure of dispersion in a distribution about its average. The variance of X is defined as variance $X = \Sigma (X_i - \overline{X})^2$ where X_i is the individual values of X and $\overline{X}$ is the average value of X.

groups. For example, suppose for both blacks and whites the distribution of genes or the genetic effect for IQ is that given in Fig. 5.1, which is centered around a score of 90. Next suppose that blacks and whites have the distribution of environmental effects, which by assumption have a smaller variance than the genetic effects, as portrayed in Fig. 5.2. The black and the white environmental distributions are constructed to have the same variance, but whites have a higher average level of environment ($\overline{N}$). In Fig. 5.3, the com-

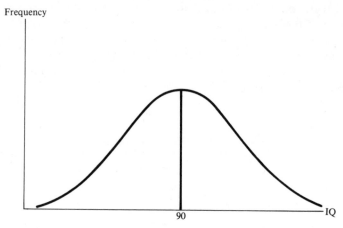

Fig. 5.1 Hypothetical Distribution of Genetic Effects on IQ for Whites and Blacks.

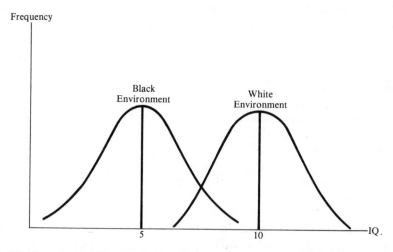

Fig. 5.2 Hypothetical Distribution of Environmental Effects on IQ for Blacks and Whites.

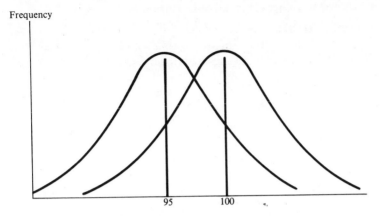

Fig. 5.3 Distribution of IQ for Blacks and Whites.

bined effects of genetics and environment are shown. By construction, whites have a higher average IQ solely because of their higher average environment. Also by construction, within the groups of white or black the contribution of environment to the variance of IQ is relatively small. Thus, evidence about the relative variance of G and N does not indicate anything about $\bar{G}$ even if the IQ measures are not culturally biased.

The IQ debate has also been heated because some people have suggested that if most of the variation in IQ is attributable to genetics, then either it is difficult to alter IQ or society has been given a signal not to alter IQ. The second position is a value judgment—one with which the author does not agree. The first position is not correct logically. If every parent chose to give his children the same environment, there would be no variation in environment. If suddenly all parents were to give a new environment, IQ could alter. For example, in Fig. 5.2 everyone could have an environment of 5, then shift to 10. In this case, the mean of the distribution in Fig. 5.3 would shift from 95 to 100, though all the variation before and after the shift would be due to genetics. In terms of income, this point can be made even clearer. The government can redistribute after-tax income through taxes and transfers, and it can institute such a policy regardless of whether the source of the variation in pretax income is genetics or environment.

The major question is not whether the government can offset genetic effects but if it chooses to do so. As noted at the beginning of this book, such a choice involves a tradeoff between equity and efficiency. To the author one aspect of equity involves the source of the earnings inequality. In the author's view society can and should help those unfortunate enough to have been endowed with, or reared in a family environment which produces low earnings capacity.

1. Parents and Earnings Capacity of Offspring

Parents can affect the earnings capacity of their offspring in a number of ways. Except for mutations, their offspring's biological makeup (genes) is determined by their parents' genes.[3] Biological parents usually, though not always, rear the child. Whoever rears the child provides food and clothing; an intellectual, emotional, and physical atmosphere; and other goods and services. In providing this childhood environment parents employ their income, time, love, and affection. Parents can also affect the child's environment by the choice of neighborhood, by the number and spacing of his siblings, by the financing of his education, and by the displaying of their own attitudes and beliefs. Parents—bearers or rearers—can also affect a child's income through the gift of financial assets (during the parents' life or after death) and through the use of connections or nepotism.

Parents are not the sole determinants of the child's environment. Even as a child, the offspring can make choices on how hard to work in school; he is also subject to random events such as accidents that affect the development of his earnings capacity. Once the child becomes independent of parental control, he can make further choices and be subjected to other influences and to random events.

Concentrating for the moment on genetic endowments and family environment, we can use the human capital model of Chapter 3 to provide an interesting way of organizing this material. Fig. 5.4 is a repeat of Fig. 3.3. In Chapter 3 we suggested that it was possible that the genetically more able may get a higher rate of return from education or that the demand curve shifted to the right with genetic endowments. It is also possible that the demand curve shifts to the right because the returns to schooling depend on certain aspects of family environment. For example, family income can be used to purchase items such as books, nutrition, and health care, all of which might increase the amount of knowledge or skills a student acquires in a given school. The supply curve also can shift because of family income.

In Fig. 5.4, let D_0 and S_0 apply to individual A and D and S to individual B. Then to maximize the PDV of expected future income A and B would invest in E_0 and E_1 amounts of schooling, respectively. Note that A's income is given by MPE_0 with a similar calculation for B. Thus, B has more schooling and a higher income than A. B receives more schooling and more income because "ability" helps determine both. As long as people with more ability also have lower borrowing costs, those with the same schooling but more ability will receive more income. Similar conclusions follow if the demand curve for education shifts because of family environment.

---

3 Genes are found at particular locations on chromosomes. At each location there are two members of each gene, one contributed by the father and one by the mother. A randomly determined member of each such gene pair of a parent is given to each offspring.

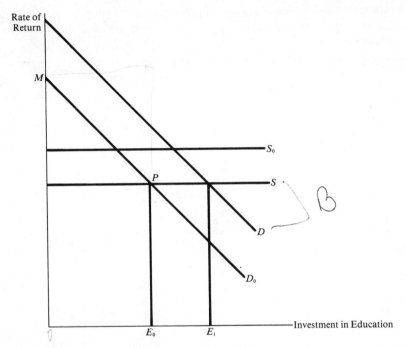

Fig. 5.4 Hypothetical Supply and Demand for Schooling.

Economists and sociologists have tried to estimate the effects of IQ and various types of family background on schooling and on earnings. A good example of this type of work is provided by Sewell and Hauser's [2] study of a random sample of 1957 high school graduates in Wisconsin.

In this study they examine effects of certain family background variables such as parental income. They estimate total, direct, and indirect effects. The difference between the three is best illustrated with an example. Suppose our model is one in which earnings depend on years of schooling, family background, and a random variable, u, as in

$$\text{Earnings} = a + b\,(\text{Years of Schooling}) + c\,(\text{Background}) + u. \quad (5.1)$$

Suppose further that Years of Schooling depends on Family Background and another random variable, v, as

$$\text{Years of Schooling} = d + e\,(\text{Background}) + v. \quad (5.2)$$

Then we can substitute (5.2) into (5.1) to obtain

$$\text{Earnings} = (a + bd) + (c + be)\,(\text{Background}) + u + bv. \quad (5.3)$$

The total effect of background is given by $(c + be)$; the direct effect is given by c; the difference, be, is the indirect effect. In Table 5.1 the first line in

Table 5.1 Effects of socioeconomic background and ability on the education, occupation and earnings of male Wisconsin high school graduates of 1957 with non-farm background

Dependent variable	Predetermined variables							
	V	M	X	I	Q	U	W	
Regression coefficients								Constant
(1) Q	.751	.481	.0326	.412				83.4
(2) U	.090	.061	.0094	.0776				10.8
(3) U	.058	.041	.0080	.0602	.0422			7.3
(4) W	1.00	.64	.136	.87				15.1
(5) W	.63	.40	.120	.67	.494			−26.1
(6) W	.19[a]	.09[a]	.060	.22[a]	.180	7.45		−80.7
(7) Y_1	−.002[a]	.012[a]	−.0026[a]	.096				5.58
(8) Y_1	−.011[a]	.006[a]	−.0030[a]	.091	.0121			4.57
(9) Y_1	−.016[a]	.003[a]	−.0036[a]	.086	.0087	.080		3.98
(10) Y_1	−.018[a]	.002[a]	−.0042[a]	.084	.0068[a]	.000[a]	.0108	4.85
(11) Y_2	.009[a]	.015[a]	.0005[a]	.122				5.96
(12) Y_2	−.002[a]	.008[a]	−.0000[a]	.116	.0152			4.69
(13) Y_2	−.011[a]	.001[a]	−.0013[a]	.106	.0084	.161		3.51
(14) Y_2	−.014[a]	.000[a]	−.0020[a]	.104	.0063[a]	.070[a]	.0122	4.50
(15) Y_3	.018[a]	.029[a]	.0006[a]	.132				6.18
(16) Y_3	.000[a]	.018[a]	−.0001[a]	.122	.0239			4.19
(17) Y_3	−.011[a]	.010[a]	−.0017[a]	.110	.0155	.197		2.74
(18) Y_3	−.014[a]	.008[a]	−.0026[a]	.107	.0129	.089	.0146	3.92
(19) Y	.018[a]	.028[a]	.0010[a]	.137				6.16
(20) Y	.000[a]	.016[a]	.0003[a]	.127	.0230			4.23
(21) Y	−.012[a]	.008[a]	−.0014[a]	.115	.0144	.206		2.72
(22) Y	−.014[a]	.007[a]	−.0023[a]	.112	.0118	.097	.0146	3.90

Source: Sewell and Hauser [2] p. 81.

Note: Item identification are: V = father's educational attainment; M = mother's educational attainment; X = status of father's occupation when son graduated from high school (Duncan SEI); I = parent's average income, 1957-1960 (in thousands of dollars); Q = son's score on Henmon-Nelson Test of Mental Ability; U = son's educational attainment; W = son's 1964 occupation (Duncan SEI); Y_1 = son's 1965 earnings (in thousands of dollars); Y_2 = son's 1966 earnings (in thousands of dollars); Y_3 = son's 1967 earnings (in thousands of dollars); Y = son's canonically weighted average of 1965-1967 earnings (in thousands of dollars). Data pertain to 2069 respondents with nonfarm background who were employed in the civilian labor force in 1964, not enrolled in school, had nonzero earnings, 1965-1967, and for whom there were data on parents income.
[a] > 05

each set of equations contains the total effects of family background. The last line indicates the direct effects of family background and of schooling and other variables.

The coefficients in Table 5.1 are estimates of unknown, true values. It is possible to calculate the probability that the unknown, true value of any co-efficient will take on a particular value. The footnote a in the table indicates that the probability is smaller than 5% that the true value is zero. This is usually described as the coefficient is "not statistically significant." Economists and other social scientists do not like to rely on coefficients which are not significant.

As shown in Table 5.1, the total effect of parental education, father's occupational status, and family income are all positive and statistically significant in equations for the offspring's schooling, IQ, occupational status, and earnings (about 7 years after high school). For example, each additional year of mother's education is associated with the offspring having 0.06 years more schooling; 0.48 points higher IQ, and $290 more earnings in 1967. Table 5.1 also traces the path by which these family background measures affect earnings and other variables. All the background measures have an impact on earnings, for example, because of their influence on schooling. Given schooling, however, only parental income has a direct effect on earnings. These particular findings for background are consistent with a number of alternative explanations. Parental education, for example, may be an indicator of different rearing techniques or different preferences for education. Parental income is presumably related to good nutrition, to high levels of education, and to other goods and services that can produce healthiness or labor market skills. These same variables may also indicate the level of genetic endowment of the parents which are related to the genetic endowments of offspring. To the extent that background variables represent genetic effects, the coefficients in Table 5.1 overstate the potential effectiveness of policies that "improve" family background.

There have been a number of studies similar in concept to that of Sewell and Hauser in which the same and other background measures have been used. Generally parental income and education are important and have positive effects on offspring's education. Number of siblings usually has a negative effect on educational attainment and earnings.[4]

This latter result is consistent with the idea that when families stretch their budget to raise more children, expenditures per child are decreased. In addition, parents may increase cognitive and other skills by spending time with, and income on, their children. With more children, parents may spend less time "training" each individual child.[5] It has also been suggested that

---

4 See Sewell and Hauser [2] or Taubman [3].

5 See Lindert [4].

the intellectual atmosphere of the family may depend on the family composition with children who come later in the birth order doing less well because their older siblings, still being children, reduce the average current intellectual atmosphere. [6]

Since educational attainment is related to earnings, the same background variables are correlated with earnings if schooling is not held constant. Once the effects of schooling are eliminated, much of the influence of background on earnings is eliminated—as was the case for parental education and father's occupation in the Sewell and Hauser study. Their results, however, are based on men with 7 years or less of work experience. Several studies suggest that later in the working career parental background measures are related to earnings even after eliminating the impact of schooling.[7] There is also some evidence that other measures of family background which may be related to motivation and drive are more important aspects of family environment for labor market success.

Family environment can be defined as all the activities and choices of (rearing) parents that affect the offspring's skills and preferences for work. It seems likely that parental education, income, and the other variables are crude proxies for family environment and may also be proxies for genetic endowments.

2. Family Studies

Recently several people have begun to approach the problem of measuring the effect of the family on offspring's achievement by using data on brothers (or siblings) reared in the same household.[8] With such data it is possible to divide the total variation in, say, income, into that occurring within and between families. The so-called within-family effect includes both genetic and family environmental effects and incorporates all the forces such as living in a particular neighborhood which make the siblings similar. But since the neighborhood is chosen by the parents, it does not seem inappropriate to attribute neighborhood impacts to the family. This family effect, however, does not include the full genetic effects, since brothers share only some of the same genes. Nor does it include the full family environment effect if parents treat each offspring differently.

These studies suggest that the family effect is much larger than that indicated by the parental education and other background variables. Olneck [8], for example, finds that the directly measured variables account for

---

6 See Zajonc and Markus [5].

7 See Fägerlind [6] and Taubman [3].

8 See Chamberlain and Griliches [7] or Olneck [8].

about 50% of his total effect (which does not include all genetic effects) of the family on earnings.[9]

A better idea of the full magnitude of the family effect is gained from data on identical twins. Recently Behrman, Taubman, and Wales [11] have published some results for a large sample of white male twins (born about 1920). Some of their results are given in Table 5.2. In this table, the within-family column is the cross-twin correlation, while the between-family column is one minus the cross-twin correlation. Behrman, Taubman, and Wales find that over one half the variation in the education and occupational success occurs within the family, with the figure being 75% for education. (Even these estimates may be understatements because identical twins need not be treated identically by parents.) They also find that a large list of family background measures, which unfortunately does not include parental income, accounts only for 20% to 25% of the total family effects. For a portion of their sample a measure of a cognitive skill is available. Holding no other variables constant, IQ can account for about 13% and 36% of the

Table 5.2 Within and between family variances for identical and fraternal twins

	Percentage of variance			
	Based on identical twins		Based on fraternal twins	
	Within Family	Between Family	Within Family	Between Family
Education	76%	24	54	46
Initial Occupation Status	53	47	33	67
Occupation Status About Age 45	43	57	20	80
Earnings About Age 50	54	46	30	70

Source: Behrman, Taubman, and Wales [11].
Note: Occupation scored on Duncan scale.

---

9 Similar results on the relative inadequacy of the usual measures of family background are found in Sewell and Hauser [2], Chamberlain and Griliches [7], Jencks and Brown [9], and Taubman [10].

variance in earnings and schooling, respectively. These figures are small compared with the total effect of the family on the same variables even though they incorporate variation in IQ that arises outside of the family.

Table 5.2 also gives within and between-family estimates for fraternal twins. Since such twins are brothers born at the same time, it is not surprising that the within, between estimates are quite similar to those derived from brothers.

The difference in results for identical and fraternal twins can be attributed to differences in either genetic endowments or in the degree of similarity of family environment of identical and fraternal twins. If fraternal twins are treated less alike because of parents' response to differences in genetic makeup, and if this same response pattern occurs for individuals in general, it does not seem improper to attribute these effects back to the genetic endowments.

Using the assumption that cross-sib correlation of family environment is the same for the two types of twins, Behrman, Taubman, and Wales have divided the family effects into genetic and family environment effects. The results are somewhat sensitive to certain assumptions. Those in Table 5.3 are intermediate in the estimate of the size of the genetic effects. In the table both genetics and family environment have noticeable impacts on all four variables with the genetic effect always being the larger. Genetic endowments effects are estimated to be somewhat larger for education and annual earnings than for occupational status. Family environment is much more important for education than for the other variables.

Table 5.3 Genetic and family environment effects

	Percentage of total variation attributable to family environment and genetic endowments	
	Family environment	*Genetic endowment*
Education	41%	36
Initial Occupation Status	31	22
Occupation Status About Age 45	29	13
Earnings About Age 50	45	12

Note: Total effects differ slightly from those in Table 5.2 because of differences in estimation techniques.

Source: Behrman, Taubman, and Wales [11].

Table 5.3 is based on a particular set of assumptions. Other assumptions, which leave the total family effect unchanged, can increase the genetic contributions by about 20% or decrease them to zero. The latter estimates require that the cross-sib correlation in environment be about 0.95 for identical twins and 0.60 for fraternal twins and that this difference not be attributable to parents' responding to genetically based differences and similarities. Personally the author finds it difficult to believe that there is such a marked divergence in parental treatment of identical and fraternal twins unless parents react strongly to genetically based differences.

The above results partition the variance in earnings, schooling, and occupational status to genetic endowments and family environment. These results, however, do not indicate what skills or capabilities are derived from these two sources. Behrman, Taubman, Wales, and Hrubec [12] have used some information for a subset of the sample to calculate the effects of cognitive skills on these variables and the extent to which the family affects cognitive skills. They find, for example, that in an earning equation IQ has a large, statistically significant coefficient, but that IQ explains no more than 13% of the variance in earnings. They also find that the family accounts for about 80% of the variance in IQ. Thus, much of the effect of the family and of genetics must flow through noncognitive skills and characteristics.

Both the genetic and the environmental correlations between parent and child may be influenced by a variety of "institutional" and other arrangements which in turn may be affected by a variety of tax policies. Some of these arrangements include who marries whom, rules governing financial inheritances, and decisions on family size.

Marriage patterns can be important for both the genetic correlation and the distribution of financial inheritances. Marriage patterns can be affected by a wide variety of social policies, including rules specifying groups who are and are not marriageable (e. g., miscegenation laws), income tax laws, and subsidization of college education. Suppose, for example, in choosing a marriage mate, people try to maximize their own utility which is dependent on the mate's physical and emotional characteristics and productivity in both the household and the marketplace. Individuals generally don't examine all 1-½ to 2 trillion individuals of the opposite sex in making a choice but limit it to those with whom they (or their relatives) have some contact. The subsidization of college may let different types of people meet. The income tax laws generally apply only to market earnings. Thus, with a progressive income tax, a person with a high market earnings potential and high tax rate would find it more profitable to marry someone with better home productivity, everything else being equal.

The rules governing financial inheritance that economists have examined are those that detail how estates shall be divided up. That is, shall all offspring share equally; shall the eldest son receive all or a disproportionately large share; shall males and females share equally; and what proportion of the estates shall be given to nonfamily members, including charity? Again, society can influence these choices, for example, by outlawing or making mandatory primogeniture (the eldest son inheriting all). Tax regulations on estates and inheritances can also affect the distribution of financial estates.

Family size can be important for a variety of reasons. For example, when there is equal sharing of estates, the more children the wealthy have, the smaller will be inequality in wealth in the next generation.[10] Also, as was indicated earlier in this chapter, there is some evidence that suggests that larger family sizes lead to reductions in IQ, schooling, and earnings.

Economists have begun to examine some of these issues. For example, Pryor [13] and Stiglitz [14] have examined the effects of equal sharing versus primogeniture rules in models where there are no genetic effects. For any initial distribution of wealth, the models they investigated tend to end up with equal distributions of wealth except when there is primogeniture. Part of the explanation for this equality result is that when people marry without regard to their partner's wealth the average wealth in each family tends to be distributed more equally in each generation. Splitting the family fortune between several children accelerates the process.

The family effects, regardless of their partition into genetic and environment components, are large. They indicate that who your parents are is very important for determining your annual earnings, occupational status, and schooling.

These findings are reinforced by the few bits of information available about financial inheritances and nepotism. By definition, only wealthy people leave large amounts of assets. By choice they tend to leave these bequests mostly to their children or to already born grandchildren. There is some evidence that the wealthy tend to leave approximately equal shares to their children (or grandchildren), which sharing will, by itself, lessen the concentration of assets and the income they yield in the next generation.[11]

Newcomber [15] provides some evidence on nepotism. She studied a group of top managers of the largest U. S. corporations in 1950. Approximately 12% of those studied indicated that their father was the head of the same corporation. While suggestive of nepotism, this of course does not prove that these people had not earned the position by merit. Updated versions of this study have shown that the percentage of family members in the top-management group has declined over time.

---

10 However, intergenerational wealth mobility may be unaffected.
11 See Menchik [16].

3. Conclusion

In this chapter we have examined the sources of inequality in earnings. We have found that a large portion is derived from the family. We have discussed briefly how and why the family operates to cause these differences. There is some suggestion that family income, perhaps on a per capita basis, is important.

We have also examined some recent work on genetics and family environment which suggest that both components are important. These latter results, of cource, are taken from a particular sample of white males born around 1920. The little information available would suggest that comparable results are obtained for education for more recently born twins.[12] Again we remind the reader that parents can choose to alter the environment they provide their children and that society has the means to change the distribution and the relative importance of genetics and environment.

The above results on genetics and family environment, if confirmed in other samples, would indicate to me that too much of the inequality in earnings is not a reward for individual effort but is dependent on factors beyond the control of the individual. Thus, I would conclude that the distribution was inequitable and that redistribution through the provision of a better environment or through transfer programs was appropriate.

The results available in the studies of brothers and of twins indicate that "family environment" has noticeable effects on earnings. Unfortunately, these studies currently do not indicate what the relevant aspects of this environment are. Suppose, however, it were possible to equalize completely family environment and, in common language, to equalize opportunity. Then the material in Table 5.3 suggests that about 1/4 of the family effect and 1/8 of the total variation in earnings would be eliminated. These numbers are, of course, based on earnings around age 50 and may be different for lifetime earnings, but if these figures are correct, programs of equality of opportunity will have little effect on reducing inequality in income or the role of the family in creating inequality.

REFERENCES

1. Arthur Jensen. "How Much Can We Boost I,Q. and Scholastic Achievement." *Harvard Educational Review* 39: 1 – 123 (1960).
2. William Sewell and Robert Hauser. *Education, Occupation and Earnings: Achievement in the Early Career*. New York: Academic Press, 1975.

---

12 See Jencks and Brown [9].

3. Paul Taubman. *Sources of Inequality of Earnings*. Amsterdam: North Holland, 1975.

4. Peter Lindert, "Sibling Position and Achievement." *Journal of Human Resources*, forthcoming.

5. Robert Zajonc and Gregory Markus. "Birth Order and Intellectual Development." *Psychological Review* 82:74 – 88 (1975).

6. Ingemar Fägerlind. *Formal Education and Adult Earnings*. Stockholm: Almqvist and Wicksell, 1975.

7. Gary Chamberlain and Zvi Griliches. "More on Brothers." In *Kinometrics: Determinants of Socioeconomic Success Within and Between Families*, edited by Paul Taubman. Amsterdam: North Holland, 1977.

8. Michael Olneck. "On the Uses of Sibling Data to Estimate the Effects of Family Background, Cognitive Skills and Schooling: Results from the Kalamazoo Brothers Study." In *Kinometrics: Determinants of Socioeconomic Success Within and Between Families*, edited by Paul Taubman. Amsterdam: North Holland, 1977.

9. Christopher Jencks and Marsha Brown. "Genes and Social Stratification: A Methodological Exploration with Illustrative Data." In *Kinometrics: Determinants of Socioeconomic Success Within and Between Families*, edited by Paul Taubman. Amsterdam: North Holland, 1977.

10. Paul Taubman. "Earnings, Education, Genetics and Environment." *Journal of Human Resources* 11:447 – 61, (1976).

11. Jere Behrman, Paul Taubman, and Terence Wales. "Controlling For and Measuring the Effects of Genetics and Family Environment in Equations for Schooling and Labor Market Success." In *Kinometrics: Determinants of Socioeconomic Success Within and Between Families*, edited by Paul Taubman. Amsterdam: North Holland, 1977.

12. Jere Behrman et al. "Inter and Intra Generational Determinants of Socioeconomic Success, Genetics, Family and Other Environments." Mimeographed. University of Pennsylvania, 1977.

13. Frederick Pryor. "Simulation of the Impact of Social and Economic Institutions on the Size Distribution of Income and Wealth." *American Economic Review* 63:50 – 72 (1973).

14. Joseph Stiglitz. "The Distribution of Income and Wealth Among Individuals." *Econometrica* 37:382 – 97 (1969).

15. Mable Newcomer. *The Big Business Executive: The Factors That Made Him*. New York: Columbia University Press, 1955.

16. Paul Menchik. "A Study of Inheritance and Death Taxation: A Micro-Econometric Approach." Unpublished dissertation, University of Pennsylvania, 1976.

Social 6
Mobility

In the previous chapter we examined some of the ways in which parents can influence the earnings and income of their children. Some of the evidence suggests that these influences are substantial. For example, roughly half the variance in earnings at age 50 can be attributed to the family. In this chapter we will also be concerned with the connections between parents' and children's income, but in small case we shall concentrate on "social mobility".

People are concerned with social mobility for a variety of reasons. Some people feel that the system is unfair when a father's occupation completely determines his son's occupation, as might occur in a caste system. Other people argue that the vigor and healthiness of a society is related to the degree of social mobility. For example, people may work harder and be more innovative if they believe that their individual effort will be rewarded and that they are not typecast by whom their parents are. Or, alternatively, a poor person is better off if he feels that his children are not automatically condemned to poverty.

1. Definition and Composition of Social Mobility

Loosely, social *immobility* is the degree to which a child's income is the same as his parents. Social mobility, then, is the degree to which a child's income differs from that of his parents. This is often measured by the intergenerational correlation coefficient R, which is defined in the appendix to this chapter. R will be positive as long as parents' income is above the average of all parents, and their child's income is also above the average of all children.

R can range from $+1$ to -1. If R equals 1, a child's income can be predicted exactly from his parents', and there is complete immobility or no social mobility. If R equals 0, there is no (linear) relationship between child's and parents' income and complete social mobility. If $R = -1$, a child's income can be predicted exactly from that of his parents. A parent with the highest income will have a child with the lowest and a grandchild with the highest income. Thus, there is complete cyclical immobility. The further R is from 0, the smaller is social mobility.

It is instructive to consider why R is large or small. Earlier we expressed an individual's earnings in terms of genetics and environment as

$$Y = G + N \tag{1}$$

This same equation can be used for both parent and child. The correlation in Y across generations, therefore, will be an average of the across-generation correlations in G and N, as shown more formally in the appendix to this chapter. Thus, R can be altered by changing the intergenerational correlations for genetics or for environment.

The parent-child genetic correlation need not be fixed. For example, changes in marriage patterns (assortive mating) or in fertility patterns, both of which may be influenced by social policies, can alter this correlation. Suppose, however, that this correlation is fixed. R can still be altered by changing the parent-child environmental correlation.[1]

The parent-child environmental correlation can be influenced by a variety of factors. For example, the child-rearing practices experienced by a person while a child can influence choice of such practices when he becomes a parent. In addition, family income, which is probably an important element in environment, can be correlated over generations because of inheritances of money, genes, or even tastes.

2. Estimates of Social Mobility

In the previous section social mobility was defined in terms of parent-child correlations for income. There are in fact relatively few samples with information on income of parents and children. As a substitute most of the research has used the occupation of the parent and the child.

Duncan et al. [1], for example, find that for white native-born males 25 to 64 years old, the R for occupation is about 0.35, which of course is closer to 0 than to 1. There are, however, several features in this study that probably have caused the R to be understated. First of all, this R is calculated from information about the child's occupation in a given year. While in general a person's occupation is more stable than his income and while many occupations to which a person might switch have the same score in the

---

1 Changes in e^2 or h^2 can also influence R, but the effects need not be large or intuitively obvious because $e^2 + h^2$ always equals 1. Thus an increase in e^2 must lead to an equal decrease in h^2.

scaling system used, over a career many people engage in many occupations with different scores. Not only are there ups and downs from year to year, but on average occupational status like income increases with age and work experience. Thus, information on those aged 25 or so will understate their average occupation. Both of these types of variation will probably cause the R based on occupation in a given year to be less than the R between lifetime status of parent and child. In addition, the information on father's occupation is obtained from questions from the child and may be subject to large recall error which will decrease R.[2]

All the above comments suggest that the intergenerational R for occupational status is greater than 0.35. The corresponding figure for earnings, however, may be much lower for the following reason. The occupational status measures are based on both average earnings and the percentage of people with at least a twelfth-grade education in an occupation. But the variation in earnings within occupations is very large, and the correlation between occupational status and earnings for individuals is generally 0.2 or less. It seems very unlikely that both parent's and child's earnings will deviate by the same amount from the average earnings in an occupation.

The previously mentioned ongoing study [2] of 1958 high school seniors in Wisconsin provides information on parent-child correlations on income and on occupational status. The data in this sample are probably subject to less measurement error than in most studies, since income measures for both generations come from tax records and can be averaged over several years while occupation data are collected directly from members of both generations. On the other hand, the group studied need not be representative of the U. S. population or even of all those who in 1958 had children about 18 years old since high school dropouts are excluded. Moreover, the latest information on earnings for the children is for 1971, which is near the beginning of most of the children's career, a period which is often atypical of average behavior. For both occupational status and earnings, R in this sample is no more than 0.2. Again, we would expect the R for lifetime earnings to be greater than 0.2 for the reasons given in the discussion of occupational status. However, the restriction of the sample to those who are high school graduates may have inflated R.

Another way to obtain some information on the parent-child correlation on lifetime earnings is from data on siblings or fraternal twins. The parent-child correlation on earnings depends upon both the genetic and the environmental correlations between parent and child. The cross-sib correlation for siblings also depends on genetic and environmental correlations. We would expect both the genetic and the environmental correlations to be

---

2 This assumes that the error is not correlated with the true response or any measurement error on the child's occupation.

at least as large as for fraternal twins (or sibs) as for parents, offspring.[3] Fraternal twins need not follow the same career path, and they can be affected differently by the business cycle and random events. Nevertheless, at any age both such twins are likely to be above or below their lifetime average. For these reasons the cross-sib correlation in annual earnings for fraternal twins can be taken as an upper bound to the parent-child correlation for lifetime earnings.[4]

The few estimates available on R for earnings of fraternal twins or for sibs are in the range of 0.25 to 0.3. Based on these findings and the earlier results in the Wisconsin data, it seems likely that the intergenerational R for lifetime earnings is about 1/4 or less. Since this number is closer to zero than to 1, the social system is closer to complete mobility than to complete immobility. On the other hand, few poeple would have expected to find that the U. S. society is a caste system with an R of 1. An R of 0.25 indicates that parents can confer noticeable advantages and handicaps on their offspring and that a goodly portion of one generation's advantages persist in the next generation.

How big or important an R of 0.25 is can be judged to some extent in the following hypothetical example. Suppose that lifetime earnings (or more likely the log of lifetime earnings) is distributed normally in every generation. Further suppose that average earnings is constant for each generation. Then it is possible to calculate the (conditional) probability that a child will be in any third of the lifetime earnings distribution, given his parents' position in the lifetime earnings position. The results for this hypothetical example are given in Table 6.1. Consider first those whose parents were in the bottom third of the distribution. About 42% of their offspring would be found in the bottom third, while about 25% would reach the top third. Because the normal curve is symmetric, the results for those whose parents are in the top third are the mirror image. Thus, the probability that an offspring from the poorest third of the families would reach the top third is smaller by

---

3 In some genetic models the genetic correlation for parent-child is equal to that for fraternal twins (or siblings), while in other models (with dominant genes) this correlation can be greater or smaller for parent-child than for fraternal twins. However, in the sample under discussion the genetic correlation will be greater for fraternal twins than for parent-child. See Behrman, Taubman, Wales, and Hrubec [3], Chapter 8, for details. The parent-child environment correlations are almost certainly smaller than that for siblings or fraternal twins because parents and child don't share the same prenatal environment and social setting in the formative years.

4 Some idea of the difference between the cross-sib correlation for fraternal twins and the parent-child correlation can be obtained by comparing the two numbers directly for occupational status in the same sample. The parent-child correlation is about 0.15, while the fraternal twin correlation is about 0.2. For unknown reasons both these figures are lower than those obtained from Duncan et al. [1]. The difference between 0.15 and 0.2, however, still may be informative.

17 percentage points, or 68%, than the probability for the offspring of the richest third. If there were complete social mobility, each entry in Table 6.1 would have been 33⅓%, which differs by 9 percentage points from the entries in the upper- and lower-right-hand cells.

If we had used finer gradations of the income distribution, the deviations from complete mobility would be even more pronounced for those whose parents were at the very top or bottom. For example, 20% of those whose parents were in the top 10% would also be in the top 10%.

Table 6.1 Probability of an offspring being in a particular 1/3 of the distribution, given his parents's position assuming R between parent and child is 0.25

Parents	Child bottom 1/3	Middle 1/3	Top 1/3
Bottom 1/3	0.42	0.33	0.25
Middle 1/3	0.33	0.34	0.33
Top 1/3	0.25	0.33	0.42

3. Altering Social Mobility and Intragenerational Inequality

In this section we examine various policies that can be used to alter both social mobility and intragenerational inequality. A useful framework in which to explore these issues is provided by a model presented in Conlisk [4]. In our notation, his model can be expressed as

$$Y_C = A_C + e\,Y_P + u_C \qquad (2)$$
$$A_C = G_C + b\,Y_P + v_C \qquad (3)$$
$$G_C = dG_P + w_C \qquad (4)$$

where

A is "ability" scaled to have a unit coefficient
G is a genetic index scaled to have a unit coefficient
Y is income
u is a random variable
v is a random variable
w is a random variable
P is parent
C is child

The same equations are assumed to hold for each generation.

In this simplified model, a child's income depends directly upon both ability and his parents' income. His ability, in equation (3), depends directly on his genetic endowments and his parents' income. As indicated in equation (4), a child's genetic endowments depend upon his parents genes, but there are random differences since each parent only contributes one half of his or her genes. The other two equations also contain random variables, which might be luck or parts of family environment uncorrelated with family income.

Conlisk [4] calculates both the parent-child correlation in earnings and the variance in earnings, both of which are constant for all generations. Since the formulas are too complex to derive and present here, only his results will be discussed. Suppose a policy of equal opportunity were to be introduced. Such a policy might mean that variations in family income would not have as big an effect on A_C and Y_C, or that there would be a reduction in e or b.[5] Alternatively, it might be possible to reduce the variance of either u or v. Conlisk shows (pp. 83 – 85) that a reduction in b or e will reduce the intergenerational R. In other words, if family environmental effects are made less important, social immobility will decrease and social mobility will increase. On the other hand, if the random elements in environment are reduced, R, which measures intergenerational resemblance, will increase. Conlisk also shows that both policies will decrease the variance of income. Thus, if society cares about both social mobility and intragenerational income inequality, different types of policies have different implications.

A policy of equality of opportunity, as conventionally defined, could at best eliminate the parent-child environmental correlation. Some calculations in Chapter 8 of Behrman, Taubman, Wales, and Hrubec [3] indicate that such a policy would leave a parent-child correlation of 0.14 or less. This is a rather small number. On the other hand, such an equality-of-opportunity program would only reduce intragenerational inequality by about 12%. (See Chapter 5.)

It may seem surprising to the student that the contributions of genetic endowments and family environment are much different for intergenerational mobility and intragenerational inequality. But it must be remembered that all genetic diversity enters into the intragenerational measure while only the correlated parts enter the intergenerational measure. Moreover, because of the laws of biology, the intergenerational genetic correlations generally can only be much greater than $1/2$ if there is an enormous amount of assortive mating (alike mating with one another). There is no law that states that the environmental correlation could not be 1.

---

5 For example, school lunch programs could be used.

4. Summary

In this chapter we have examined some aspects of social mobility. While the data leave much to be desired, it seems that social mobility is less than complete and that children from wealthy families have a much better chance to remain wealthy than children from poor families have of becoming wealthy.

We have also seen that social mobility is not the same as intragenerational inequality of earnings and that some policies could decrease inequality within a generation but increase social immobility.

REFERENCES

1. Otis Duncan et al. *Socioeconomic Background and Achievement*. New York: Seminar Press, 1972.

2. William Sewell and Robert Hauser. *Education, Occupation, and Earnings: Achievement in the Early Career*. New York: Academic Press, 1975.

3. Jere Behrman et al. *Inter and Intragenerational Determinants of Socioeconomic Success: Genetics, Family and Other Environments*. Mimeographed. University of Pennsylvania, 1977.

4. John Conlisk. "Can Equalization of Opportunity Reduce Social Mobility?" *American Economic Review* 64:80 – 90 (1974).

Appendix to
Chapter 6

In this appendix we will define the intergenerational correlation R and decompose it into its genetic and environmental components. Let Y_P be parents' income, Y_C child's income, and $\overline{Y}$ average income. With Σ indicating the sum over all families, the parent-child correlation R is given by

$$R = \frac{\Sigma (Y_P - \overline{Y}_P)(Y_C - \overline{Y}_C)}{[\Sigma (Y_P - \overline{Y}_P)^2 \, \Sigma(Y_C - \overline{Y}_C)^2]^{1/2}} = \frac{\text{covariance of } Y_P \text{ and } Y_C}{[(\text{variance } Y_P)(\text{variance } Y_C)]^{1/2}} \quad (1)$$

Earlier we expressed an individual's earnings in terms of genetics and environment. Continuing to denote parent and child by P and C, respectively, we have

$$Y_C = G_C + N_C \quad (2)$$
$$Y_P = G_P + N_P \quad (3)$$

Then R, the correlation between Y_C and Y_P, can be expressed as

$$R = \frac{\text{covariance } G_C \text{ and } G_P}{\text{variance } G} \; h^2 + \frac{\text{covariance } N_C \text{ and } N_P}{\text{variance } N} \; e^2$$

where

$$h^2 = \text{variance } G/\text{variance } Y$$
$$e^2 = \text{variance } N/\text{variance } Y$$

Since $h^2 + e^2 = 1$, R is a weighted average. The terms multiplying h^2 and e^2 are the parent-child correlations in genetics and environment, respectively.

In deriving equation (4) it is assumed that G_C and N_P are uncorrelated, G_P and N_C are uncorrelated, the variance of G_C = variance G_P = variance G, the variance in N_C = variance N_P = variance N.

It is perhaps simpler to express equation (4) as

$$R = (R_G)h^2 + (R_N)\,e^2 \tag{5}$$

where R_G is the parent-child genetic correlation = covariance (G_C and G_P)/ variance G and R_N is the parent-child environmental correlation = covariance (N_C and N_P)/variance N.

Economic Efficiency and Costs of Inefficiency   7

In the previous chapters we have presented some material which the author believes can be used to justify the need for more income redistribution. This case will be summarized in more detail in the next chapter, which will also contain some policy recommendations. However, as pointed out in Chapter 1, nearly all programs that can be used to redistribute income will reduce economic efficiency or, in other words, cause fewer goods and services to be produced and/or the composition of goods and services to be less than optimal. The cost of these inefficiencies must be balanced against the benefits of redistribution in deciding on the best policy choices. In this chapter we will examine in more detail how a variety of possible redistributive policies cause a loss in efficiency, and we will try to put a price tag on this so-called welfare loss.

1. Economic Efficiency

In Chapter 1 and its appendix, which the student may wish to reread, we defined economic efficiency as producing the quantity and composition of goods and services with the maximum utility. We stressed that the goods and services included in this definition were not limited to those produced in the marketplace but included leisure and home-produced goods.

As we indicated in Chapter 1, in a perfectly competitive economy it is possible for consumers to maximize their utility and business to maximize their profits by using relative prices of goods and services and of factor inputs. For example, when the two goods are X and Y, the consumer maximizes utility when MU_X/MU_Y equals P_X/P_Y, which statement is a simple rearrangement of equation (1) in Chapter 1.

Both consumers and producers use relative prices to guide their decisions. Under certain conditions such as perfect competition and no taxes, there will be an efficient allocation of resources if the price paid by purchasers of a good is the same as the price received by the seller. The appendix to this chapter demonstrates why a difference between prices received and paid leads to inefficiency.

In this chapter we will examine various tax and redistributive mechanisms. A variety of mechanisms will be examined because they generate different amounts of inefficiency. The material in the appendix measures inefficiency in terms of the reduction in utility. It is difficult to determine the shape of utility functions. However, under certain conditions, including perfect competition and constancy of the marginal utility of income, it is possible to approximate this loss in utility or welfare with a much simpler technique.

Fig. 7.1 contains the supply and demand curve for market consumption. Suppose the tax imposed on market consumption is $1. Then, since the producers will require a $1 higher price to supply any amount, the supply curve will shift up by $1 to S_1. In Fig. 7.1 the equilibrium market consumption will be reduced from C to A. As shown in more detail in the appendix in Figs. 7.7 and 7.8, the reduction in market consumption means an increase in the quantity of leisure. The utility or welfare loss is given (approximately) by the area of the triangle ABC in Fig. 7.1, which is, of course, $1/2 (AB) (AC)$. Since $AB = 1$, the welfare loss is $1/2 AC$, but the length of AC depends on the angle at A or, in other words, on the slope (or elasticity) of the demand curve at this point. The steeper or more inelastic the demand curve, the smaller the welfare loss.

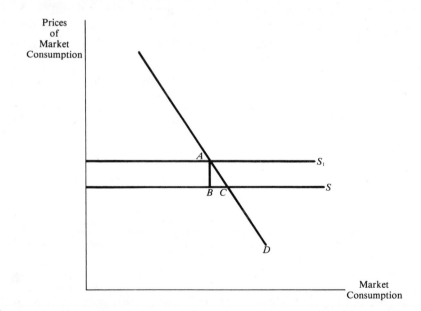

Fig. 7.1 Approximate Welfare Costs of Consumption Tax.

Both the mechanism chosen to finance income redistribution and the rules that describe the redistributive process can cause inefficiencies. The alternatives, then, can be contrasted in *terms of economic inefficiency* by comparing the areas of the various plans' *ABC*s. We will start the analysis by considering various taxes.

2. Welfare Loss of Various Taxes

The most commonly used taxes in the United States are those levied on income, consumption and wages. The theoretical literature on taxes often contrasts these with each other and with a head tax of X per live person. By definition tax revenues equal $\bar{t} B$ where $\bar{t}$ is an average tax rate and B is the revenue base. In comparing the welfare losses from these systems, it is necessary to consider both what is and is not included in the base and the size of the average tax rate. The comparisons are generally made for "equal-yield" tax systems, that is, ones that generate the same revenues.

Consider first income and consumption taxes. In both instances, we will be discussing tax systems that do not include nonmarket activites. By definition Income equals Consumption plus Savings. When saving is positive, an income tax has a larger base and smaller $\bar{t}$ than an equal-yield consumption tax. Since an income tax is levied on wages and on returns from stocks, bonds, and other financial capital, an income tax imposes a double burden on savings. That is, an income tax first reduces funds available for saving and then taxes the yield from saving. A consumption tax does not involve the second burden on saving—as is more formally demonstrated in the footnote.[1] Both income and consumption taxes affect labor-leisure choices, though an equal-yield income tax has a smaller effect because its tax rate is

---

1 Assume that an individual plans to leave no bequests and will consume all his income, Y, in his lifetime. Let there be two periods, 0 and 1. Let the quantity and before-tax price of consumption, which is the same in both periods, be C and P, respectively. Let r be the interest rate, t the income tax rate, and v the consumption tax rate. With an income tax, the two-period budget constraint is:

$$[Y_0(1 - t) - PC_0] [1 + r(1 - t)] + Y_1(1 - t) - PC_1 = 0 \qquad (1)$$

With a consumption tax, the two-period budget constraint is

$$[Y_0 - PC_0(1 + v)] [1 + r] + Y_1 - PC_1(1 + v) = 0 \qquad (2)$$

In both equations saving in the first period is the term in the first square brackets. The ratio of after-tax price of consumption in periods 0 and 1—as viewed in period 1—are given in equations (3) and (4) for an income and a consumption tax, respectively.

$$1 + r(1 - t) \qquad (3)$$
$$(1 + r) \qquad (4)$$

In other words, an income tax lowers the price of present versus future consumption and affects saving decisions. A consumption tax is neutral, since equation (4) would hold when there were no taxes.

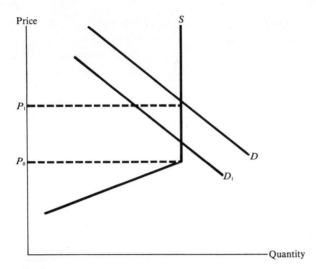

Fig. 7.2 Economic Rent.

smaller. Thus, an income tax causes more distortion in saving decisions and less in labor-leisure decisions than an equal-yield consumption tax. Which of the two involves greater welfare losses can only be determined empirically.

Though structured in an entirely different way, analytically a wage tax is like a consumption tax in that it induces inefficiency in labor-leisure choices but not in consumption-saving choices. If there is no inherited wealth, over a lifetime a wage tax and consumption tax would have the same base and average tax rate. When there is inherited wealth, the two taxes need not have the same base, but which base is bigger depends on whether initial inheritances are greater than subsequent bequests.

The inefficiency associated with the tax system examined above occurs because individuals, who can make choices, do not have vertical demand (or supply curves). It might be asked if there is some tax system which has no inefficiencies associated with it. There are several systems which have this property. For example, consider Fig. 7.2, which can refer to hours worked or to any commodity. In this figure the supply curve becomes vertical at P_0. The demand curve intersects the supply curve at P_1. The difference between P_0 and P_1 is defined as "economic rent"; the increase in price from P_0 to P_1 does not induce any extra supply. Now suppose a tax of $t\%$ were imposed on the sale of this item. After the imposition of the sales tax, less would be demanded at any pretax price; in other words, the demand curve would shift to D_1. With this shift, the price would fall by the amount of the tax, and since the same supply would be forthcoming there would be no welfare loss. Unfortunately, since it is very difficult to identify commodities or individuals with economic rents, this tax system is not very practical.

A lump-sum tax is one in which a person has to pay a fixed amount. The most commonly analyzed lump-sum tax system is a per capita tax, which is in fact used in some communities in the United States. Unfortunately, a per capita tax can cause inefficiency because people can choose to die and, more importantly, to have or not have children. Leaving aside issues connected with death, a lump-sum tax imposed solely on adults would not cause inefficiency. But such a tax is generally considered so unfair as to be impractical for the nation as a whole.

3. Labor-Leisure Choices

We have indicated that a tax on market consumption or income will cause individuals to substitute leisure and nonmarket consumption for market goods. The mechanism by which this substitution takes place is a reduction in time and effort spent working in the marketplace. Since total time can be divided only between leisure and marketplace work, the demand for leisure can be restated in terms of the supply of hours to the marketplace. (Both hours worked and intensity of effort may be affected by tax laws. We will discuss intensity shortly.) The student who wishes to study in more detail this substitution process should turn to pages 90-94, where certain redistributive mechanisms are examined. But at this point, the empirical estimates of the sensitivity of hours worked to changes in tax rates will be discussed.[2] Sensitivity is based on the estimated change in hours worked as after-tax wage rates vary (but with income held constant).

Consumption and other taxes can influence an individual's decision to work at all in the marketplace (to participate in the labor force) and can help determine how many hours labor-force participants wish to work. The available evidence would suggest that labor-force participation for males age 25 to 54 is about 98% and is not sensitive to variations in tax rates—when the tax rate is not close to 100%.[3] However, for younger and older males and for females, groups which contain a majority of working-age persons, labor-force participation is far from universal and is sensitive to variations in tax rates.[4,5]

---

2 Much of the relevant empirical material in this and subsequent sections is ably surveyed in Break [1].

3 For a recent summary see Cain and Watts [2]. Tax rates at or near 100% are found in certain special programs, examples of which are described below.

4 See Cain and Watts [2].

5 Since nearly all men in prime ages work, a woman's choice on participation can be thought of as the marginal decision. Because income tax rates are based on family income, a wife can face a very high tax rate. The total income tax and social security tax rate on the first dollar of a wife's wages can easily be 40% to 50%.

While much of the available evidence on hours worked would suggest that variations in tax rates (not close to 100%) would have little effect on hours worked of participants, there are studies that reach the opposite conclusion.[6] Since there are enough flaws in all the studies, it is difficult to reach any firm conclusions on hours worked of labor-force participants.[7]

Hours worked and intensity of effort are not the same thing. It is possible that consumption or other taxes will induce individuals to expend less effort per hour worked or to be less willing to undertake to train for occupations with more responsibility. There are, however, no studies which have tried to estimate the size of such reduction in effort in response to tax-rate changes.

In summary, it appears that the labor-force participation rate for a majority of the working-age population is somewhat sensitive to variations in tax rates. The evidence on hours worked and intensity is too inadequate to make a judgment as to sensitivity. However, the participation result indicates that there will be a noticeable welfare loss from taxes used to finance additional income redistribution. Suppose an increase in taxes of $10 billion was necessary. This would induce a loss in welfare (from labor-leisure choices) of probably no more than $15 billion, or 1% of the gross national product.

4. Consumption-Saving Choices

Besides labor-leisure choices which have just been discussed, an income tax affects consumption-saving choices. As indicated in the footnote on page 82, the income tax affects consumption-saving choices by altering the interest rate from r to $r(1 - t)$. Thus, to determine the sensitivity of saving to income taxes, it is necessary to examine only the coefficient on $r(1 - t)$ in a consumption or saving equation which contains other appropriate variables such as current and future after-tax income.

During the past 30 years there have been many studies which have estimated the consumption function, but it is astonishing to report that very few of these studies have included $r(1 - t)$ or even r in the analysis. [8,9]

---

6 See Hauseman and Wise [3].

7 Most of the studies have been concerned with wage rate effects and have not adjusted for taxes.

8 For some exceptions see Wright [4] and Boskin [5].

9 It is beyond the scope of this chapter to consider in detail why interest rates have not been included, but one reason is that most people apparently believed that either the coefficient was near zero or that r did not vary enough to explain movements in saving or the saving, disposable income ratio. In addition, many of the studies were concerned with other major issues such as the proper allowance for corporate saving and undistributed profits, the shifts in age composition, and the impacts of changes in the social serurity system.

While many economists believe that interest rates have almost no effect on saving, a recent study by Boskin [5] finds that a 1% increase in the after-tax interest rate (from say a tax decrease) would raise saving by about 0.5%. Boskin's study, however, treats the data differently than many others. For example, he adds corporate saving to personal disposable income and personal saving on the grounds that corporations are owned by people and that individuals should be indifferent between a dollar saved directly by themselves or indirectly by their agents. Some people would dispute this proposition and his results.

While definitive information is not available on this subject, there is some weak evidence that the author thinks supports the contention that after-tax interest rates have only small effects on saving. In recent years the U. S. tax laws have been changed so as to enlarge the number of individuals who can accumulate much of their retirement funds while postponing paying taxes till after they retire on both the pension fund contribution and its earnings. For many individuals who will not retire for 20 or more years and who are currently in a 30% to 60% marginal tax bracket, this postponement will effectively reduce the tax to perhaps 15% or less and will increase greatly the after-tax interest rate. As far as the author is aware, there has been no marked increase in saving resulting from this change. Thus it may be that there is no large welfare loss arising from distortion on consumption-saving choices. This conjecture is reinforced when it is recalled that the interest on Series E bonds need not be counted as income till the bonds are cashed. Thus, the effective tax rate on these bonds was very low, but the interest rate on these assets was very close to those on taxed saving accounts. Moreover the difference in the interest rates between Series E bonds and savings accounts did not vary as taxes changed, as would happen if savings were related to interest rates.

5. Income Redistribution Mechanisms

Society has available a large number of mechanisms by which it can redistribute a given amount of income among its members. The rules that describe each redistributive mechanism will determine the losses in economic inefficiency additional to the above ones connected with the financing mechanism. The two broad mechanisms used are those that increase earnings capacity by the acquisition of skills and those that transfer money or commodities directly. In both categories, determining eligibility is an important consideration.

Society can increase a person's income by augmenting his skills. It was argued in Chapter 3 that an individual who wished to maximize the *PDV* of his lifetime earnings stream should invest till the rate of return on his investment equals the interest rate on borrowed funds. This same argument also implies that some people don't acquire skills because the rate of return on the investment is too low. Society can induce such individuals to acquire more skills by lowering the cost of the investment or by reducing the interest rate on borrowed funds through direct loans or guarantees.

Education is one way to increase skills. Even the most pessimistic results reported in Chapter 4 still indicate that each additional year of schooling increases earnings by 3%. Governments already provide incentives to people to acquire college education through guaranteed loans, fellowships, and scholarships, and through tuition and fees set lower than costs in public institutions.[10] In addition, public and private colleges administer privately contributed endowment funds which are used for scholarships and to lower tuition and fees below costs.

The inefficiency connected with these programs is twofold. First, while the government subsidizes colleges and some approved vocational schools, not all potential training institutions are subsidized. Thus, the subsidies will induce some individuals to obtain training that has a lower rate of return to society. Moreover, some people may still choose not to enter any of the subsidized programs because the rate of return remains too low. These people won't be helped by such programs. Put another way, a reduction in borrowing costs to 7% won't induce those who benefit least from schooling—have a lower than 7% return—to obtain schooling. This latter group seems likely to be the poorest.[11]

The last argument may sound like it is based on equity rather than on efficiency considerations. But an important aspect of fiscal or redistributive efficiency is to obtain the maximum amount of redistribution from a given expenditure. This brings us to the second problem with skill subsidization. There is a substantial difficulty in setting up rules so that the subsidies will be given only to those who were poor or would not acquire the skill without the subsidy. As partial steps in this direction, scholarships and government-guaranteed loans are often related to family income. Even here, however, there are problems. It has been successfully argued that college students who are adults are independent of their parents; hence, in calculating "need," the amount of the scholarship, and so on, only the student's own low current income is used. Moreover, setting tuition and fees below costs benefits all students, including those who would have acquired college at an unsubsidized price.

Next, let us consider various income transfer schemes. There are a variety of income transfer programs which share the characteristic that the

---

10 The government may be doing this because it believes there are externalities, such as a better functioning democracy, that raise the social return above the private return. But these policies affect the income distribution.

11 The literature on who benefits from government subsidies to colleges is extensive but not in agreement. See Hansen and Weisbrod [6] for one view and Pechman [7] for another.

amount of the transfer is dependent on the individual's labor market earnings. For example, it is generally acknowledged that payments made to the elderly by social security are partially a transfer from younger workers. In other words, these payments are more than would have been made from a private pension or annuity system that had to break even. A person eligible for social security payments need not retire, but if he works and is less than 72 years old, then the following formula comes into play. Until his earnings reach $3,000, his social security benefits are unchanged. Above that amount each dollar of his earnings reduces his social security benefits by 50 cents until his benefits are reduced to zero.[12] This 50% reduction in benefit is called the implicit tax rate. Put another way, the social security system imposes an implicit tax of 0, 50%, or 100% on earnings, with the actual rate dependent on the earnings level.[13]

As a further example, payments made under the various state welfare systems consist of an initial grant which is reduced as earnings increase. Other important programs in which the amount of benefits depends upon earnings or family income include: Aid for Dependent Children (AFDC), Medicaid, food stamps, basic opportunity grants for education, and certain types of housing assistance.[14]

Aaron [8] has calculated the tax rate on earnings of a family with two dependent children eligible for the Aid for Dependent Children, Medicaid, food stamps, and housing assistance.[15] His results, which are given in Fig. 7.3, indicate that the tax rates on earnings are "high and capricious." The tax rate is often as high as 80%. He provides an even more extreme example. In the figure the marginal tax rate drops sharply above $8,390 because at that point the family is no longer eligible for AFDC, Medicaid, and food stamp benefits. Thus, the tax on earnings increasing by $1 from $8,389 to $8,390 is about $1,300.

The various provisions in these programs cause different losses in economic welfare. To explain why the particular provisions have such different costs it is necessary to describe and analyze certain basic forms of the provisions.

A transfer system can be described in terms of the initial grant of income, the implicit tax rate on income or earnings, and other eligibility rules. The systems described in Table 7.1 all involve an initial grant and different implicit tax provisions, of which that in item 4 requires the most comment.

---

12 The rules are more complicated since for example, eligibility is determined on a quarterly basis. If a person lumps his earnings into one quarter, he could receive his benefits in the other three quarters.

13 The person is also liable for state and federal income taxes on earnings.

14 For an excellent summary of most of these, see Aaron [8], Chapter 2.

15 See Aaron [8], especially Chapter 4.

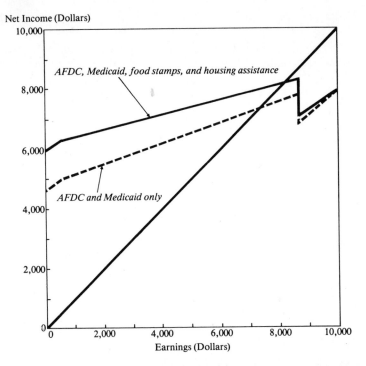

Fig. 7.3 Value of Disposable Cash Resources Plus In-kind Benefits for Family of Four under Aid for Families with Dependent Children, for Two Combinations of Benefits, by Earnings Level, 1972. (*Source:* Aaron [8], p. 34.)

In some transfer programs, a person is eligible for full benefits if his income (or assets) is below a certain level but eligible for no benefits if his income is equal to, or greater than, this level.

Table 7.1 A variety of transfer systems

Description	Examples
1. Transfer, with no "tax" on earnings	Social security benefits for those over 72
2. Transfer, tax on earnings	AFDC, Social security for those less than age 72
3. Transfer, tax on family income	Food stamps, housing assistance
4. Transfer, tax 100% or 0%	Medicaid rules in certain states

The various panels in Fig. 7.4 portray the different schemes in Table 7.1 To aid in the analysis, it is useful to introduce the concepts of a budget line and an expansion path. Suppose an individual receives utility from market-produced goods (and services) and from leisure time. Let the price of market goods be 1, the market wage rate be w, and the tax rate be t. The budget line indicates the opportunities an individual has for consuming leisure and goods. An individual who gives up one more hour of leisure will receive $w(1 - t)$ dollars of earnings which can be used to buy $w(1 - t)$ dollars' worth of goods. Thus, the slope of the budget line is $w(1 - t)$. If the individual has no income from sources other than earnings, the budget line will start at the point in the graph at which leisure equals 24 hours a day and income (or goods) equals zero, that is, at Q in Fig. 7.4a. If the person has other sources of income of $\$AQ$, the budget line will start at the point such as A in Fig. 7.4a.

To maximize utility the individual selects that point on the budget line at which the combination of leisure and goods is such that the MU leisure/MU goods $= w(1 - t)$. The position of the budget line depends upon the size of nonwage income, AQ. Imagine there being a change in AQ to CQ in Fig. 7.4a, but with the after-tax wage rate unchanged. Then the budget line would shift to CD, which is parallel to AB. Along CD there will be a point at which MU leisure/MU goods $= w(1 - t)$. The line OP, which is called the expansion path, connects the points on all parallel budget lines at which the ratio of the marginal utilities equals $w(1 - t)$. OP need not be a straight line and, in some cases not considered here, need not be sloped upward. However, since it is assumed that both goods and leisure are subject to diminishing marginal utility, at points above and to the left of OP, MU leisure/MU goods must be greater than $w(1 - t)$.

Now let us examine Fig. 7.4a in detail. Assume initially that the person is in equilibrium at M along AB. Next, suppose we give the person a transfer grant of $\$C\text{-}A$. Now when he works 0 hours, a person's income will be $C\text{-}Q$. Thus, the new budget line CD will begin at C, have a slope of $w(1 - t)$, and be parallel to AB. The optimal point on CD will be at N where CD intersects the expansion path, since by definition the expansion path indicates the point on each parallel budget path where $w(1 - t)$ equals the ratio of the MU of leisure and income. As the figure is drawn, the individual reacts to the transfer by taking more leisure and working fewer hours, which result we have obtained before. This figure, however, can help us understand some additional aspects of economic inefficiency. In Fig. 7.4b the grant $C\text{-}A$ is large enough so that CA intersects the expansion path OP. Since the ratio of the MU's to the left of OP is greater than $w(1 - t)$, at no point on CD can the ratio of the MU equal $w(1 - 1)$. The individual will find his greatest utility at C where he works 0 hours. Thus with a large enough grant, the individual will drop out of the labor market.

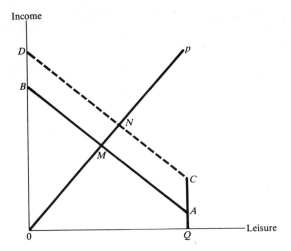

Fig. 7.4a Transfer System with No Tax Provisions.

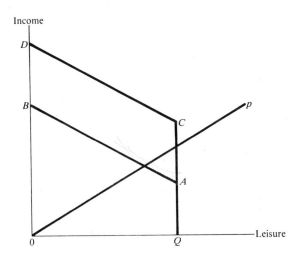

Fig. 7.4b Transfer System with No Tax Provision and a Large Grant.

Now let us consider the effects of tying the transfer payment to earnings. Suppose the grant consists of C-A if the individual has zero earnings, is reduced to $0 if the individual earns $5,000, and is reduced by $s\%$ (where s is less than 100%) for each dollar earned between $0 and $5,000. (The case of a 100% tax rate is considered in Fig. 7.4d.) This system is shown in Fig.

7.4c. Here the after-transfer budget line begins at C, then has a less steep slope than AB (because of the reduction in the grant as earnings increase) and intersects AB at D. For income above \$5,000 the transfer is 0 and the initial budget line applies.

Fig. 7.4c contains two hypothetical expansion paths, OP and OP^1, because the impact of the transfer system depends on the position of the expansion path relative to the point D. Consider first OP which intersects AB to the right of D. In this segment of the graph, the transfer system will be effective in the sense that it will redistribute income but will cause inefficiency. The amount of the inefficiency is not obvious in the graph but can be described. If the slope of CD were the same as that of AB, the optimal point would be at E. But since CD is flatter than AB, the optimal point must be on CD and to the right of OP.[16] However, if the expansion path is OP^1, the transfer system is ineffective in transferring income but causes no inefficiency. In a system such as that described in Fig. 7.4c it would be expected that some people would be on OP and have their income raised while others are on OP^1.

In some transfer systems such as food stamps the amount of the grant depends on family income rather than on earnings. Fig. 7.4c can be easily modified to encompass this situation. The point C would be set at the initial grant minus the repayment $s(A - Q)$. The rest of the diagram would be unaltered.

In some transfer systems eligibility depends on the level of pretransfer family income or earnings, but there is no implicit tax on earnings if the person remains eligible. The situation is as portrayed in Fig. 7.4d. Eligibility ceases at an income level of D. Thus, the budget line including the transfer jumps discontinuously from D to E and consists of $CDEB$. If OP passes between E and D, the person would find that his best point would be at D, which has as much income and more leisure than E. Such an "all-or-nothing" eligibility system contains a substantial incentive not to work.

Fig. 7.4d can also be used to analyze the case where the grant is reduced dollar for dollar of earnings till the net transfer falls to zero. That is a system in which the transfer has an s of 100% on earnings till some maximum earnings after which s falls to zero. In terms of Fig. 7.4d, the points C and D would coincide, and the budget line would still have the discontinuity from C to E. Once again there would be substantial incentives for people not to work.

In general it is fair to conclude that transfer systems will cause people to substitute leisure for income and result in economic inefficiency. Moreover,

---

16 That is, the lower after-tax and transfer wage rate causes people to substitute more leisure for income than would be chosen in Fig. 7.4c with a grant that would cause CD to go through the point E.

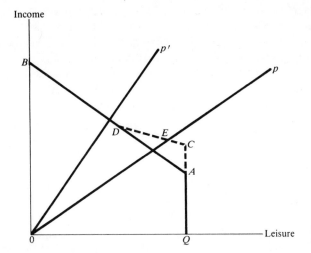

Fig. 7.4c Transfer System with Tax on Earnings.

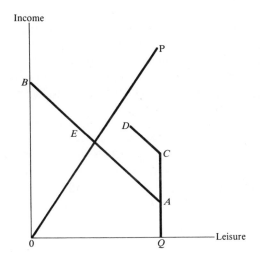

Fig. 7.4d Eligible, Noneligible Transfer System.

transfer systems which reduce benefits as earnings (or income) increase will result in greater inefficiency, with the amount of inefficiency increasing with s, the implicit tax rate on earnings.

There still remains the question of the magnitude and welfare loss of these inefficiencies. The reduction in hours worked or increase in leisure arising from various transfer schemes can be divided into an "income" and a "substitution" effect. The income effect is the reduction in hours worked as income increases, but the slope of the budget line, $w(1 - t)$, is unchanged. Thus, the change from M to N in Fig. 7.4a is an income effect. There is no welfare loss from an income effect because relative prices to producers and consumers are unchanged (ignoring the losses from financing the transfer). The substitution effect is the change in leisure as the slope of the budget line shifts but income is constant. The transfer systems portrayed in Fig. 7.4c and 7.4d contain substitution effects, though the sizes of the effects are not shown. The magnitude of the substitution effect depends on the slope (elasticity) of the supply-of-labor curve, the empirical evidence on which was discussed earlier.

In recent years several variants of a negative income tax scheme have been advocated as a supplement to, or wholesale replacement for, the existing plans. In one basic version of the negative income tax scheme, each family of four is granted, say, $4,000, but each dollar of earnings reduces the grant by 33⅓ cents till the grant reaches zero, at which point earnings are $12,000. This proposal is essentially the one given in Fig. 7.4c which applies to existing programs like food stamps and Aid for Dependent Children. However, the proposed ⅓ tax rate on earnings is lower than those contained in AFDC or food stamps. The reduction in the tax rate has two important consequences. First the lower the tax rate, the smaller is the substitution effect and welfare loss. Second the lower the tax rate, the higher is the income level up to which families receive a transfer payment and the more dollars transferred. That is, if the negative income tax reduced the grant by 50 cents of each dollar earned, only families with incomes up to $8,000 would receive benefits. This plan would cost less both because fewer families would be eligible and because smaller payments would be made to families at each income level (provided there were not too large a reduction in labor supply). While the version of the plan with a 50% tax rate would cause more economic inefficiency *among recipients* than the 33⅓% version, the latter would require higher taxes, which has its own efficiency cost. Thus, it is not clear which of these is more inefficient.

6. Conclusion

In this chapter we have examined why transfers lead to inefficiency and have tried to calculate the cost of such inefficiencies. The inefficiencies arise because either the financing or the rules governing the transfer alter the relative prices for labor and leisure or consumption and saving and cause the relative prices to differ for individuals and businesses, the demanders and suppliers of services and goods. The inefficiencies clearly exist, but the available empirical work is not definitive enough to pinpoint the welfare losses. However, it was suggested in the section on financing that a $10 billion tax increase would cause a welfare loss no larger than $15 billion or no more than 1% of the GNP. Even allowing for all the other welfare costs discussed in this chapter, it is hard to believe that the loss in welfare from a $10 billion increase in transfers is more than 2½% of the GNP, which is approximately the annual growth in per capita GNP (in constant dollars).

REFERENCES

1. George Break. "The Incidence and Economic Effects of Taxation." *The Economics of Public Finance*. Washington, D. C.: The Brookings Institution, 1974.

2. Glen Cain and Harold Watts. *Income Maintenance and Labor Supply*. Skokie, Ill.: Rand McNally, 1973.

3. Jerry Hausman and David Wise. "The Evaluation of Results from Truncated Samples, The New Jersey Income Maintenance Experiment." Mimeographed. Kennedy School, Harvard University, 1975.

4. Colin Wright. "Saving and the Rate of Interest." In *The Taxation of Income from Capital*, edited by Arnold Harberger and Martin Bailey. Washington, D. C.: Brookings Institution, 1969.

5. Michael Boskin. "Taxation, Saving and the Rate of Interest." *Journal of Political Economy*, forthcoming.

6. W. Lee Hansen and Burton Weisbrod. *Benefits, Costs and Finances of Higher Education*. Chicago: Markham, 1969.

7. Joseph Pechman. "The Distributional Effects of Public Higher Education in California." *Journal of Human Resources* 5:361 – 70 (1970).

8. Henry Aaron. *"Why Is Welfare So Hard to Reform?"* Washington, D. C.: Brookings Institution, 1973.

Appendix to
Chapter 7

In the appendix to Chapter 1 we introduced production possibility frontiers and indifference curves, which will now be reproduced for the reader's benefit. In Fig. 7.5 the production possibilities curve AB indicates all the possible combinations of brussels sprouts and beefsteak that can be produced *when labor, capital and other resources are fully utilized*. The social indifference curve indicates all the combinations of the two goods which yield the same level of satisfaction or welfare to society. That is, society is indifferent among all the points on I_0. Along I_1, there is more welfare since any point on I_1 has as much beefsteak and more brussels sprouts as at some point on I_0. For the same reason indifference curves cannot intersect. We remind the reader that there is only a unique social indifference curve if everyone has the same tastes; otherwise income redistribution may alter the shape of indifference curves. We will assume here, however, that redistribution does not alter the indifference curves.

The combination of beefsteak and brussels sprouts that yields the most satisfaction or social welfare is found at the point where AB just touches, or is tangent to, an indifference curve. (As long as AB is smooth and concave from below and the indifference curves do not intersect one another, there will be only one tangency point.) In Fig. 7.5, the combination that yields the most satisfaction, the optimal point, is M. Any other combination is not optimal, or is inefficient.

It is "easy" to see the optimal point in Fig. 7.5, which has only two goods. In the real world, however, there are many goods, and the production possibility curve and the indifference curves are not known. Still, it may be possible to reach a point like M. For example, under certain conditions, including perfect competition, no taxes, and no "externalities" such as pollution, the information contained in relative prices is enough to drive

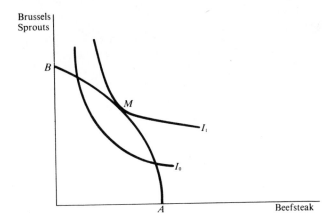

Fig. 7.5 Production Possibilities Curve.

profit-maximizing business and utility-maximizing individuals to M. That is, in Fig. 7.5 business goes to the point on AB where its slope is equal to the ratio of the prices, while consumers go to the point on I where its slope is equal to the ratio of the prices. If the price ratios facing consumers and businesses are the same, the economy will reach M.

Suppose, now, that the government levies a tax of $t\%$ on the producers of brussels sprouts. If P_B is the price consumers pay for brussels sprouts, producers will receive $P_B (1 - t)$. The relevant relative prices for producers and consumers in Fig. 7.6 are given by P_1 and P_2, respectively. Continue to assume that businesses maximize profits and consumers maximize utility. Consumers and producers who now face different prices will find that in Fig. 7.6 the combination of goods at R, where P_1 is tangent to AB and P_2 is tangent to $I_0 I_0$ will yield them the most utility and profits, respectively. The point R, however, has less utility than M.

In Fig. 7.6 it was assumed that the tax was levied on only one of the goods being consumed. Such taxes, often called excise taxes, are employed in the United States. However, most tax revenues in the United States are obtained from more general taxes such as those imposed on income or consumption. Suppose, for example, the government levied a tax of $t\%$ on all goods produced for sale to consumers (i. e., goods made by a business and purchased by consumers). In this instance relative prices to consumers and producers would be the same for these goods, and it might seem that there would be no inefficiency. But consumers can obtain utility from goods or services not produced in the marketplace. For example, consumers can forgo work (and thus the income to buy beefsteak or brussels sprouts) to enjoy leisure, or they can produce meals at home in part using their time rather

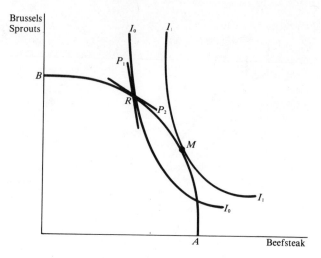

Fig. 7.6 Effects of Tax on Brussels Sprouts Producers.

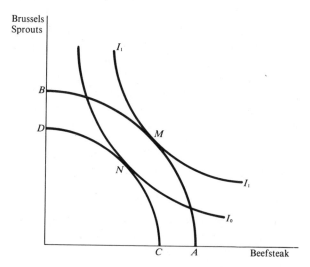

Fig. 7.7 Effects of a Consumption Tax Where Leisure Is Not Taxed.

than buying them at a restaurant. In other words, a consumption tax reduces the amount of labor available for market production. Since the production possbility frontier's position depends on the amount of labor and capital available, the increase in leisure time will move the production possibility frontier for market goods inward, as to *CD* in Fig. 7.7.

The difference in results in Fig. 7.6 and 7.7 (movement along AB or a shift to CD) is an artificial one that arises because we are using only two-dimensional graphs. To see this, note that we can in Figure 7.6 analyze the two goods consisting of (1) consumption of all goods and services bought in the marketplace and (2) leisure merely be relabeling brussels sprouts as consumption and beefsteak as leisure. Thus, using either Fig. 7.6 or 7.7, a tax on market-produced consumption will induce an individual to substitute leisure for market consumption and will create inefficiency. From either figure we can calculate the cost to society of the inefficiency as the difference in utility or social welfare between the pre- and post-tax equilibrium points, that is between M and either N or R. As is most clearly seen from Fig. 7.6, the reduction in utility comes about because the composition of market consumption and leisure is not optimal. Thus, the cost of the inefficiency is not the reduction in market consumption but the difference in the utility of the leisure substituted for market goods.

Conclusions and   *8*
Recommendations

Throughout this book we have examined why it is that individuals and families earn different amounts. It is necessary to know why people have different amounts of earnings in order to be able to say what the consequences of various policies would be and to decide on whether more or less redistribution is required. A judgment on the need for more (or less) redistribution and the mechanism by which redistribution should be channeled should be based both on the aggregate level of economic welfare and on the relative fairness of its distribution before and after implementing a policy. The following represents the author's judgment on both the need for redistribution and the mechanisms to achieve redistribution. These judgments are based on personal beliefs on equity and incomplete information on efficiency issues. Even reasonable students could reach different conclusions.

Currently some, perhaps many, people believe that the existing mechanisms to redistribute income and the associated taxes needed to pay for such redistribution have given rise to substantial losses in economic efficiency and to a large group of "welfare cheaters." The latter group are often thought of as those who are capable of work but instead choose to stay at home and be supported by the overtaxed, hardworking middle class. Sometimes the concept of welfare cheaters is extended to people who expend some minimum effort in the marketplace but substitute public support for more extensive work effort. Finally, welfare cheaters include those who gain transfer payments by outright fraud; for example, by filing multiple welfare claims under different names or by claiming more children than they have.

As shown in the previous chapter, economic theory indicates that people will have an incentive to substitute public support for private work effort. And while not analyzed formally, it can be shown that when crime pays some people will resort to it—whether the crime be robbery, fraud on welfare claims, cheating on income tax returns, or obtaining defense contracts by bribery.

Undoubtedly, there is fraud and some substitution of public dole for private effort. Accurate information on how extensive either type of "cheating" is, is hard to come by, though some people have guessed that 5% to 10% of welfare recipients are receiving payments to which they are not legally entitled though many of these errors are caused by administrative mistakes rather than by fraud. As we will see, it is possible to redesign some policies to reduce these activities. For example, the government could transfer income only by subsidizing training or education which increase future earnings. Such a policy should be subject to less fraud than transfer systems with benefits dependent on earnings. It would also be possible to curtail "cheating" by eliminating or reducing income transfer schemes. This latter alternative would be more attractive if it were true that a large proportion of people on welfare were capable of earning an adequate living or of moving above the poverty line. We can use the material in the earlier chapters to examine some of these issues.

Much, though not all, of the existing income redistributive programs go to people with low incomes and to those below or near the poverty level. As shown in Chapter 2, the people still living in poverty are to a very large extent those who are elderly, mentally or physically handicapped, or women who are heads of households with children at home. Clearly, some of these people are capable of working, and indeed there are blind persons or women heads of household who work and support their families with little or no government support. There are mechanisms, described below, that can encourage some people in this category to work more, but it is difficult to believe that society wishes to tell the elderly and infirm that they do not deserve to receive societal support or to tell mothers that they should not care for their children, especially if day-care centers are not available.

Of course food stamps, Medicaid, and other income transfer programs often go to those above the poverty line. For many such recipients there is a feeling that they are capable of earning much more than they are currently. Yet we have seen in previous chapters that variation in income (or earnings) in this country is not trivial. For example, in 1971 the average income in the lowest and top fifths in the income distribution was $2,800 and $25,700, respectively. (Since then prices have risen more than 70% and incomes have risen by about the same percentage.) This nearly 10 to 1 ratio also understates the relative positions of those in the top and bottom 5% or 1%.

Moreover, we have seen that nearly all males aged 25 to 54 are working or looking for work. For these men, annual hours worked are at least 1,600, for nearly everyone who is not unemployed much of the time and variations in wage rates have little effect on hours worked. Moreover, poor people work. Studies indicate that among heads of poor families one-third are working full-time and at least one-sixth part-time.

We have also seen that much of the inequality in earnings arises because of the family in which one is born and raised. For example, around age 50, about 57% of the variance in earnings is attributable to the family. Such family effects can occur because skills and characteristics are inherited genetically, are inculcated by parents, or are dependent on family income. The 57% due to the family can be subdivided into 45% and 12% for genetics and family environment, respectively—though the division into these components is subject to more error and uncertainty, especially since these estimates are based on one point in the life cycle from a single sample which itself is not a random drawing of the U. S. population.

Still, if these estimates are at least approximately correct, they suggest that the life chances of a person are tightly circumscribed by the skills and characteristics produced by the family. Of course, since the previous chapters have not identified what skills and characteristics—other than IQ—produce earnings, one of the personal charateristics may be willingness to work hard. Yet at least for men participation rates and hours worked would indicate substantial work effort. Moreover, the author personally would find it difficult to deny income transfer payments on the grounds that one of these *unknown* characteristics may be willingness to work hard—especially if such a characteristic resulted from forces beyond the individual's control.

The results on sources of inequality have another implication. In most equality-of-opportunity programs, the focus is on eliminating differences in prices and/or in tastes associated with family environment. (Elimination of discrimination, which is based on genetic characteristics, is an exception.) If it is true that approximately 10% of the inequality in earnings is attributable to family environment, then even if it were feasible to eliminate all such inequality of opportunity, the variance in earnings would not be much reduced and the family would still count for 45/88, or about one-half of the remaining inequality (though social mobility would be very high). It is worth noting that the method by which the family effect of 57% is split into the genetic and environment components attributes to genetics that unknown proportion of family environment that is dependent on the offspring's genetic endowments. That is, if parents deliberately provide more resources to those children who are more genetically able because these children make better use of these resources, the method counts this as arising from genetic differences. Thus, it is not possible to say what would happen if, for example, all offspring were treated exactly alike or if all children were raised in day-care centers or in something like a kibbutz.

Chapter 4 began with a discussion of the changing view of the importance of education in creating inequality and its potential role in eliminating inequality. Most recent studies have found that after controlling for age and certain family background characteristics, each year of schooling adds 8%

3 %

to 10% to annual earnings. When, in addition, cognitive skills are held constant, the effect of education declines between 5% and 30%, with the small decreases occurring when people with only a few years of labor experience are studied. Often in these samples, education accounts for up to 25% of the variance in annual earnings. However, more recent studies using twins and siblings have generally concluded that the observed effect of schooling mostly reflects uncontrolled-for differences in ability and family background. For example, Taubman [1] finds that within pairs of identical twins, each additional year of education may add 4% or less to schooling. Using a coefficient of this magnitude, schooling would account for no more than 5% in the variance in earnings.

As emphasized in the human capital model, in a competitive market some of the variations in annual earnings is induced in order that the rate of return on investment in schooling be equalized to the interest rate. There is some indication that education would explain a higher proportion of the variation in the present discounted value of lifetime earnings, but using Lillard and Willis's estimate that 75% of the variation in annual earnings is the variation in permanent earnings, education per se can explain less than 6% of the variance in lifetime earnings.

There are reasons to suspect that a major shift in the level and distribution of schooling would cause the wages associated with various education levels to alter, but suppose we ignore this. Then, a policy to equalize education would result in no more than a 6% reduction in the inequality of lifetime earnings. Such a reduction is not trivial, but it obviously leaves a substantial amount of inequality. In principle, the remaining inequality could be overcome by a compensatory education program in which the less able students were given more years of education or more educational resources than the more able students. Even leaving aside the question of how the more and the less able students are to be selected, and ignoring the question of whether our model is correct when it is stretched to say that the least able students can benefit from four years of college and a Ph.D. program, the amount of compensatory education needed is huge. For example, the difference in average earnings between the top and bottom fifths in 1971 was nearly 800%. Even if each year of education added 10% to earnings, the bottom fifth would need an extra 80 years of education or equivalent resources to catch up with those in the top fifth. Of course this is a silly example in that some of those in the bottom fifth have low incomes because they are unemployed or out of the labor force. But if our results that each additional year of education adds 4% or less to earnings is correct, compensatory education cannot be very effective.[1]

---

1 It is also possible that more educated workers take more of their increased labor market productivity in the form of nonwage payments, which would cause us to understate the impact of education on a truer measure of economic welfare.

This is not to say that education is unimportant or an unwise invest-ment. Education, it is often argued, affects people's performance in, and enjoyment of, many activities outside the labor market. Returns in the form of better parenting, more efficient allocation of household resources, better citizenship, or better appreciation of works of art are real returns. Since it is difficult to quantify these returns, no one can really say what is the total rate of return to investment in schooling. But, as argued above, there is sub-stantial evidence that schooling per se does not have a big impact on the in-equality in earnings.

It is possible, of course, that other training programs are more effective than formal schooling in reducing inequality. At this stage of our knowl-edge, however, it is difficult to say what these training programs—if there are any—are.

Programs to encourage schooling and other training programs can be justified on the grounds of equalizing opportunity by eliminating market imperfections or on the grounds of equalizing outcomes by instituting com-pensatory programs. Income transfers can also be used to equalize out-comes. Such transfer programs can be used regardless of whether the reason for the existing inequality is genetic or environmental.

As indicated in Chapter 7, the United States already has many transfer programs with a variety of benefits and with various implicit tax rate sched-ules which are tied to income or wealth. There are several major difficulties related to transfer systems. These problems, which are interrelated, include: the costliness of the program; the number of people covered; the implicit tax rate schedule in the transfer program; and the management of the pro-gram. For example, if a transfer system gives each person who does not work $1,000 but reduces the grant by 50% of each dollar of earnings (the implicit tax rate), the labor supply of people who can earn less than $2,000 (the break-even point) will be affected; and indeed some people with earn-ings greater than $2,000 could decide to work less and enjoy more leisure. On the other hand, if the program were designed so as to give, say, $1,200 with a tax rate of 80%, the break-even point would be $1,500. Assume that these two programs cost the same dollar amount if no one were to alter their labor supply. But under the second plan people would have more of a ten-dency to substitute leisure for income, and the plan would involve different costs to the Treasury and the taxpayer. Such differences would affect in-come tax rates and involve the economy in other inefficiencies. Clearly, as the level of the initial grant at zero hours of work increases, people with low incomes receive more and the opportunity to substitute leisure for income will be extended further up the income scale.

Direct transfer outlays can be saved if potential recipients are identified by characteristics other than income. For example, suppose it is felt that ev-eryone should have an income or its equivalent of at least $4,000 and it is known that any nondisabled person can earn $2,000 a year at the minimum wage rate. A grant of $3,000 with, say, an implicit tax rate of one half would allow anyone to receive at least $3,000 plus the option of working and receiving at least $1,000 more. (Any able-bodied person could always work full-time and receive $3,000 plus one half [$2,000].) However, a handicapped person who could not earn $2,000 a year would not be able to receive $4,000 or its equivalent. Obviously, raising the $3,000 grant to $4,000 would allow everyone to have an income of at least $4,000. But this increase in the grant would cost more funds. An alternative policy is to give $4,000 to those who are unable to work but the original $3,000, 50% tax rate plan to everyone else. This policy will involve less direct transfer payments but may necessitate a monitoring and management program to insure that only those who are truly unable to work receive the $4,000. Such a management program involves monetary costs for wages and paper, and nonmonetary costs such as invasion of privacy.

Based on the above considerations, I would advocate a two-tier transfer program to help equalize a distribution that I consider too unequal and arising from indefensible sources. Every family should be eligible to receive an amount at least equal in value to the poverty level, which is not a generous level of income.[2] Those who are above the age of 65; are blind, deaf, or certified as disabled; or families with only one adult worker with children not in high school may choose to be in a program with a grant equal to the poverty level and with a reduction in the grant of one-third for each dollar earned. In addition, the grant net of repayment will be included in the income tax base and subject to additional tax if *taxable* income is positive. (Currently for a family of two who are not above 65 and are not blind or deaf, taxable income would be positive if gross income were about $5,000.)

Everyone in the society would also be eligible for the following program—though no one could participate in both. First, every family would receive a grant equal to one-half of the poverty line. This amount would be included in taxable income. Second, each person would receive a supplement to his wage and salary earnings of 10%. This supplement would also be added to taxable earnings. At the same time all other existing transfers of income and consumption goods and services would be eliminated—except for a catastrophe medical insurance policy which covers all annual costs above 25% of taxable income. Also, minimum wage rates and the personal exemption on the income tax would be eliminated. Both policies would be paid for by an across-the-board increase in income taxes.

The general transfer policy of one-half of the poverty line plus a wage supplement of 10% is designed both to guarantee a minimum income to all and to encourage people to work by increasing the returns from work. Of

---

2 The Supplemental Security Income Program, in effect since 1972, already does this for the elderly.

course, this program will increase the amount of dollars transferred unless there are huge savings from the elimination of a number of separate transfer systems each with its own monitoring and management costs. The burden of financing this increase in transfer systems will fall primarily on those with nonlabor earnings and with relatively high marginal tax rates.

Given that people are to be granted a guaranteed minimum income and that the worst handicapped can opt for higher benefits, there would seem to be less reason for other transfer payments except to cover catastrophes. Similarly, the personal income tax exemption would serve little purpose, and a minimum wage would no longer be required to lift a person out of poverty.

There are several advantages to this system as opposed to increasing transfers through the current system. First, by replacing the large implicit tax rate in most current transfer systems with a 10% subsidy, people who receive benefits will have stronger incentives to work. In many cases, for example, the swing will be 60% from a tax rate of 50% to a subsidy of 10%. Second, the replacement of the current piecemeal system in which numerous people interpret various rules with one or two programs with relatively simple rules should increase the probability of equal treatment for equally situated individuals, cut down on management and monitoring costs, and should allow easier assessment of the adequacy and costs of the transfer system. Third, the system will tend to concentrate the transfers on the poor and will be less likely to have situations as currently where Nelson Rockefeller qualifies for a tax-free transfer from social security.

How much would such a system cost? It does not seem worthwhile to price it out exactly, especially since much of the relevant information is not readily available. Some rough estimates indicate that the basic grant in the two systems would probably cost about $125 billion, while the 10% subsidy would run perhaps another $100 billion.

The sum of $225 billion is quite large, but it also overstates the net additional funds required from the government. To begin with, this $225 billion would be included in taxable income. This increase in the tax base along with elimination of the personal exemption under current tax schedules would probably yield between $130 to $160 billion. Perhaps $10 billion more would be offset by the reduction in existing transfer programs. Also monitoring and management costs—wages, paper, file cabinets, and office space—at the federal, state, and local government levels could well be reduced another $15 to $20 billion. Finally, the added work incentives may well add another $5 to $10 billion in total government revenues. This would leave a net cost of perhaps $30 to $60 billion, or 2% to 4% of the gross national product. The increase in tax rates to finance this would also involve economic inefficiencies that might have a value of an additional 2% to 4% of income—since most of the labor-leisure inefficiencies discussed in Chapter 7 will be offset by the 10% subsidy rate. Is it worthwhile to incur costs of 4% to 8% of the GNP or several years' growth in GNP per capita to eliminate poverty and reduce inequality in this country? Given the earlier findings on why inequality occurs and the profile of those in poverty, I think it is.

REFERENCES

1. Paul Taubman. "Earnings, Education, Genetics and Environment." *Journal of Human Resources* 11:447 – 61 (1976).

Index